THE
WESSEX
RIDGEWAY

Also available:
The Cotswold Way
The Dales Way
The Saxon Shore Way
The West Highland Way
The Two Moors Way
The Southern Upland Way
The Heart of England Way
The Wye Valley Walk
The Cumbria Way

RECREATIONAL PATH GUIDE

THE
WESSEX RIDGEWAY

ANTHONY BURTON

Photographs by Mike Williams

Aurum Press

Ordnance Survey

First published 1999 by Aurum Press Limited,
25 Bedford Avenue, London WC1B 3AT,
in association with the Ordnance Survey.

Text copyright © Anthony Burton 1999
Maps crown copyright © Ordnance Survey 1999
Photographs copyright © Mike Williams 1999

Ordnance Survey and Travelmaster are registered trademarks and the Ordnance
Survey symbol and Explorer trademarks of Ordnance Survey, the national
mapping agency of Great Britain.

A catalogue record for this book is available from the British Library.

ISBN 1 85410 613 9

Book design by Robert Updegraff
Printed and bound in Italy by Printer Trento Srl

Cover: *The imposing ramparts of Hambledon hill fort.*
Title page: *The Wessex Ridgeway crossing Manton Down.*

CONTENTS

Circular walks will be found on pages: 48, 84, 98, 112, 136 and 138

How to use this guide

This guide is in three parts:
- The introduction, historical background to the area and advice for walkers.
- The path itself, described in eight chapters, with maps opposite each route description.

This part of the guide also includes information on key places of interest as well as a number of related short circular walks. Key sites are numbered in the text and in the maps to make it easy to follow the route description.
- The last part includes useful information such as local transport, accommodation,organisations involved with the path, and further reading.

The maps have been prepared by the Ordnance Survey® for this guide using 1:25 000 Explorer™ maps as a base. The line of the Wessex Ridgeway is shown in yellow, with the status of each section of the path – footpath or bridleway for example – shown in green underneath (see key on inside front cover). These rights of way markings also indicate the precise alignment of the path at the time of the original surveys, but in some cases the yellow line on these maps may show a route which is different from that shown by the older surveys, and in such cases walkers are recommended to follow the yellow route in this guide. Any parts of the path that may be difficult to follow on the ground are clearly highlighted in the route description, and important points to watch for are marked with numbers in each chapter, both in the text and on the maps. *Some maps start on a right-hand page and continue on the left-hand page – black arrows (➡) at the edges of the maps indicate the start point.* Should there have been a need to alter the route since publication of this guide for any reason, walkers are advised to follow the waymarks or signs which have been put up on site to indicate this.

DISTANCE CHECKLIST

The list will help you in calculating the distances between places on the Wessex Ridgeway, whether you are planning your overnight stays, or checking your progress

Location	Approximate distance from previous location	
	miles	*km*
Marlborough	0	0
Avebury	6	10
Devizes	10 ¹/₂	17
Urchfont	5	7.5
West Lavington	5	7.5
White Horse	9	14.5
Heytesbury	9 ¹/₂	15.5
Hindon	7 ¹/₂	12
Ludwell	9 ¹/₂	15
Tollard Royal	3 ¹/₂	6
Iwerne Courtney	8	13
Shillingstone	3	5
Giant's Head	12 ¹/₂	20
Sydling St Nicholas	6	9.5
Maiden Newton	2 ¹/₂	4
Lower Kingcombe	3	5
Beaminster	8 ¹/₂	13.5
Lambert's Castle	11 ¹/₂	18.5
Lyme Regis	6 ¹/₂	10.5

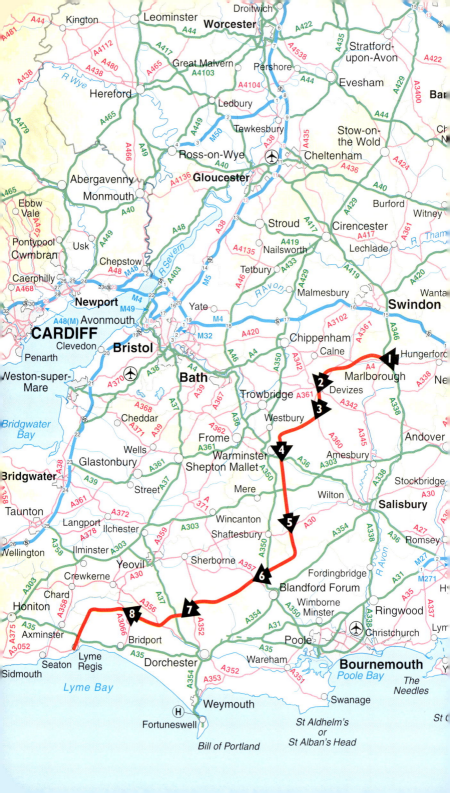

INTRODUCTION

Looking north from the path after the climb to the escarpment edge at Charlton Down.

WALKING THE WESSEX RIDGEWAY

The name of the walk suggests long sections of airy walking over high ground, enjoying wide vistas and stunning views, and this is happily true of much of the way. If, however, the would-be walker imagines a climb up to some high ridge which is then followed for mile after mile, then it has to be said that that is a very long way from actuality – some might say that a more accurate name would be the Wessex Switchback. Even where the route does fundamentally stay with an escarpment edge, as in the long walk round the rim of Salisbury Plain, it never keeps to just one level, but constantly dips and climbs. This may be disappointing for those who look for an easy life, but it has many compensations. It means that this is a walk of great variety. The valleys have their own pleasures and charms, and each climb brings a new landscape into sight. Those who walk this way will not only be aware of the major changes involved in moving from one area to another, but can also look forward to constant small changes, ensuring that each section has its own identity and offers its own delights.

Although, as explained in the notes on geology and scenery that follow, the main theme is chalk downland, it presents itself in very different ways as the route progresses. It appears first as the slow rise and swell of the Marlborough Downs, which push out into a ridge that extends down to the Vale of Pewsey. This provides a comfortingly gentle introduction, but it soon gives way to the more demanding slopes that form the edge of Salisbury Plain, particularly to the south where it is crinkled by deep valleys, producing an effect like a well crimped apple tart. Beyond that, even a quick glance at the 1:50 000 map of the region shows tight-packed contour lines wriggling and squirming across the route. This section also involves walking round the busy Army firing range – and it is somewhat unnerving to hear the noise of artillery and suddenly be confronted by an armed platoon all wearing gas masks just when you were enjoying what you thought was an empty landscape and blissfully pure, unpolluted air. On reaching Dorset, the pattern changes once again. The long ridges and escarpments become broken up into individual hills and secluded, seemingly forgotten valleys – and the hills retain this relentless rise and fall all the way to the coast. This may not be a mountainous walk, such as one might find in the Scottish Highlands, there are no dramatic rock faces, no scree slopes, no very long climbs to great heights, but the succession of stiff, short climbs ensures that the Wessex Ridgeway does offer a real challenge, and one which is richly rewarded.

The difficulties of this walk depend to a very great extent on the weather. There is very little road walking, and the rest of the way can be roughly divided between upland and lowland. At its best the upland walking is simply superb and never better than when the path scarcely exists and the walker can simply stroll along on a cushion of soft turf, enjoying the views. The ways up to and down from the heights, however, are very different. In fine weather, they

The modern church gate at Tollard Royal: the fish motif is appropriate for a church dedicated to St Peter.

seem from a distance to be white streaks painted over the hillside, revealed up close to be chalk paths sunk down to the bed rock. In the rain, however, they take a very different character, as the white turns to grey and the firm path develops the consistency of lumpy porridge. A similar story can be told of the walk in the valleys. Much of it is through and over farmland, often making use of bridleways. These do not have to get very wet before horses' hooves churn them into deep mud, which is especially true of the many woodland paths. Bridleways do not create the biggest problems. Parts of the route use byways, open to vehicles. The new popularity of off-road driving means that these can be deeply rutted, containing as much as a foot of muddy water. This, of course, represents the very worst conditions likely to be encountered, and even at the worst the tracks are still perfectly walkable, but one has to be prepared to be slowed down by the mud and there is absolutely no point in even trying to keep clean.

The comments above are intended to show what could happen, but even if the going is hard and the conditions dreadful, this remains one of the really great long distance walks. But the very qualities that make it so enjoyable also add to the problems. There are few things better than a walk over high downs on a glorious day, with the world spread towards limitless horizons and the skylark carolling your progress. But this very openness means that if a storm does break, there is probably nowhere to go to escape it. When the wind blows the rain in your face at the top of the downs, it is easy to understand the gloom that overtakes so many characters in Thomas Hardy's novels. It is true of any long distance walk that the only sensible approach is to think of the very worst that the weather can do and come prepared for it. If the worst never happens then nothing is lost. Those who blithely hope for the best can be in serious trouble if their optimism proves unfounded. When walking the route taking notes for this book, the author faced just the sort of conditions on one day that one hopes to avoid. It was on Salisbury Plain that the wind rose to gale force with showers alternating between rain and hail. Estimates of time to be taken for that leg of the journey were abandoned, and the waterproofing and windproofing of clothing was given a severe test.

The Wessex Ridgeway, then, is not a walk to be taken lightly, but good planning should help to ensure that it is a success. The first question that always has to be answered is the direction the walk should take. The description here is from Marlborough to Lyme Regis, for two reasons. It eases the walker in gradually at the start, and somehow arriving at the coast makes for a satisfying conclusion. Then one has to decide how long to take, and here two factors again come into play. Most experienced walkers have a pretty good idea of the distance that they can comfortably cover as a daily average. In general, it is sensible to err on the side of caution; far better to have extra time for investigating things met along the way or simply sitting down to admire the view, than to be worried about getting to the next stopping place in time and feeling too tired to take in anything much along the way. A week, which includes the two weekends, should be quite sufficient to allow travel to and from the way and an average walk of around 15 miles a day. The other determining factor is the availability of accommodation. One of the main delights of this walk is the way in which it keeps so very much to the open countryside, but that inevitably means comparatively few visits to villages let alone towns. Those who want a roof not canvas over their heads and a meal prepared by someone else, will often find it necessary to make a short detour. And in many stretches where a high level lasts for a long way, this may mean a walk down from a ridge and a morning that starts with a stiff climb. Ideas on how to find accommodation are given at the back of the book, and it would certainly be unwise to rely on finding somewhere en route by chance. There will also be days when the only food and more importantly drink, will be what you carry with you.

An idea of the sort of terrain encountered along the way has already been given, perhaps enough to indicate that anyone setting out along the Wessex Ridgeway should come prepared for anything. Boots are preferable to walking shoes, and are essential if the weather gets really bad. Good waterproof clothing is also required to cope with any downpours that might occur – particularly as they always seem to arrive just after the last vestige of shelter has been left behind. Route finding really splits into two sections. In Wiltshire, waymarks in the form of a roundel with a dragon at the centre, do pop up along the way, but not always in the places where they are needed, such as track junctions. They are, in any case, seldom accompanied by directional arrows, so at the best all they do is provide confirmation that you are still on the right route. Once the border is crossed into Dorset, waymarking is notably better. The same insignia are used, but now appear at most junctions and where necessary will give an indication of the direction to be followed. There is no need for concern, in any case, as the maps and directions given in the following pages should provide all the information needed. Even so, it is always a good idea to carry a compass. No one wants to walk with a head permanently stuck in a book, and it is always possible to miss a turning point. If it does nothing else, the compass will provide a useful check that you are still travelling in the right direction, and can be very useful where there is a multiplicity of tracks at a junction. And directions, however carefully written, cannot deal with all eventualities. It is all very well reading an instruction to head for the gate opposite or a marker on the horizon, but what if fog comes down and gate and marker are invisible? The compass is then the only reliable guide.

It is, of course, easy to think up a long list of what can go wrong and finish up too nervous to leave your own front door. In practice even the worst experience will not be a total catastrophe. The

A chance for walkers to cool their feet at the end of the Way: the beach at Lyme Regis.

Looking down at the modern army camp from the ramparts of the Iron Age fortress of Battlesbury Hill.

advice offered here should be thought of simply as a means of ensuring that all walkers get the maximum possible enjoyment out of the walk and there is not much pleasure in being lost, cold and wet. So a word of reassurance at the end. As mentioned, the author did not enjoy the best of conditions when walking the Ridgeway in preparing the book, but at the end could still vote it as being one of the best, most enjoyable and scenically most exciting of Britain's long distance footpaths.

NATURAL HISTORY

Think of chalk downland and one thinks at once of close-cropped turf. The dominant grass is sheep's fescue, which is indeed a popular part of the sheep's menu, but it also includes plantain, which can lay its leaves flat on the ground to avoid the munching jaws. The most spectacular flowers are undoubtedly the orchids, each species relying on its own particular kind of insect for pollination. The spotted orchid for example attracts the bumble bee, while the pyramidal orchid relies on butterflies and moths. These are not the only colourful plants that one might expect to see however, Bird's foot trefoil and horseshoe-vetch are common, and very similar in appearance, their bright yellow contrasting with the more delicate shades, varying from pale blue to pink, of common milkwort. All these attract a wide range of insects, including the increasingly rare local species, the chalkhill blue butterfly.

The survival of this lovely habitat depends on the constant grazing of sheep and rabbits. There are now fewer sheep on the downs and disease has radically reduced the rabbit population, though walkers on the Ridgeway might not think so. As a result, tougher plants such as tor grass spread rapidly, crowding out more delicate species. Unless the young shoots are nibbled away, shrubs such as hawthorn will become established and scrub will spread across the slopes and once established it is not easily removed. It does, however, bring benefits of its own: the young bushes provide an ideal stage for the yellowhammer to give a recital of its well known song, popularly given as 'a little bit of bread and no cheese', and for the even more melodious woodlark. The greatest threat to the downland comes from the farmer, who, thanks to modern fertilizers, is able to exploit even the thin upland soils. In recent years, more and more land has gone under the plough.

The lower slopes and the valley floors have a very different plant life. Cowslips and ragwort are found in the damper ground, for example, and woodland becomes more common. The beech is the tree most commonly associated with the chalk, and many of the beechwoods are blanketed by bluebells by late Spring. Walkers will find a rich variety of plant life all along the Wessex Ridgeway, but one important group can easily be overlooked. Fyfield Down is a National Nature Reserve not because of its beautiful flowers, but because the sarsen stones are home to a particularly rich selection of lichens.

Walkers over downland will certainly be aware of bird life, even if the birds themselves are not seen immediately. The song of skylark

The undulating Dorset landscape, dotted with ponds and woods, seen from Bulbarrow H

and meadow pipit have much in common, as both birds have the habit of singing their way up from the ground and changing tune as they sink down again. Their fluid song contrasts with the harsh call, like two stones being banged together, which gives the stone chat its name. Many birds will appear along the way as the habitat changes, from pheasants strutting through the woods to buzzards mewing high over the hills, but animals are rather rarer. Along with the numerous rabbits, there is the occasional hare. Foxes go about their business with their usual air of aloof superiority, and there is a very good chance of seeing roe deer, either peering out from among the trees or, in the early evening, browsing on adjoining fields. Walkers who stay out late may catch sight of a badger emerging from its set.

ARCHAEOLOGY

The Wessex Ridgeway offers a feast for those with a taste for archaeology, and the first course is served up right at the beginning of the walk. Fyfield Down is dotted with massive stones, known as 'grey wethers' from their similarity to grazing sheep when seen from a distance. These are the sarsen stones which were hauled down the hillside to Avebury to form part of Britain's largest henge monument. Built over 4,000 years ago in the Neolithic or New Stone Age, this is an immense site, large enough to contain most of the modern village. A circular ditch was dug, originally as much as 9 metres deep and the excavated chalk was piled round it in a great bank, creating a 427 metre diameter ring. Inside this was a circle of sarsen stones, nearly a hundred of them originally, with two smaller rings inside that. There are four entrances, the one to the south opening on to an avenue of stones leading down to The Sanctuary. This has been destroyed, but it seems there was originally a wooden house, presumably used for rituals, later replaced by stone circles. Nearby are massive mounds, known as round barrows, which may be of later date. There was originally a second avenue to the west, roughly along the line taken by the Way which led to The Longstones or burial mounds. Avebury was obviously a site of the greatest importance, but there are two other very impressive Neolithic sites in the area.

Silbury Hill is the largest manmade prehistoric mound in Europe. It stands over 40 metres high, and estimates suggest that it would have taken 500 workers ten years to complete. Legend has it that King Sil was buried here, decked in gold armour and mounted on his horse. The truth is no one is really sure why it was

The enigmatic mound of Silbury Hill, though made over 4000 years ago its purpose still remains a mystery.

built, though it has at least been radio-carbon dated to 2145 BC. Nearby is West Kennet Long Barrow. This is a burial mound over 100 metres long, with an impressive entrance of upright stones and a curved forecourt. Inside, a stone-lined passage leads to smaller burial chambers. Not all these sites lie on the Way, but all can be visited by taking the Circular Walk described on page 48.

Moving forward in time, and along the walk, one arrives at many examples of round barrows, the majority of which date from the Bronze Age. These can be simple circular mounds, or can be complex, with surrounding ditch and bank. Advancing again to the Iron Age brings yet more spectacular sites, the hill forts. There are eight important examples along the Way, all of which follow the same basic pattern. The sites have clearly been chosen for their strategic importance, with steep slopes providing a natural protection. The summit was then fortified with bank and ditch,

Visitors exploring the stone-lined burial chamber of the West Kennet Long Barrow, built in the New Stone Age.

usually with complex twisted entrances. One of the most interesting is Hambledon Hill, but the Iron Age settlers were not the first to come here. By the fort, the Way passes a Neolithic causewayed camp, a ritual site dating back nearly 5,000 years, with a ditch and bank, the former holding large numbers of human bones. The fort itself is vast, with double ramparts and ditches and turned entrances. It looks out across the valley to Hod Hill fort, which was later adapted by the Romans for their own fort.

There are few important Roman remains along the Way, though inevitably Roman roads cross the route. One of the more interesting is followed for about a mile over Morgan's Hill between Avebury and Devizes. This road breaks the well-known saying of all Roman roads running straight and true, for its builders wisely decided to put a kink in it to go round Silbury Hill. There is one famous monument generally thought to be Romano-British, the Cerne Abbas Giant. He is said to represent Hercules, which would place him around the 2nd century AD when worship of the god was encouraged by Commodus, who declared himself to be Hercules' earthly reincarnation. There is little doubt that the figure was a fertility symbol: the evidence is, to say the least, obvious. The figure can be reached by the walk described on page 112.

WESSEX

Historical Wessex has no exact boundaries – they changed and shifted with the fortunes of war – but the area through which the walk passes always lay near the heart of the kingdom.

Wessex is, as the name suggests, the kingdom of the West Saxons. The invading Anglo-Saxons did not march in unopposed. A stern defence was put up by the British under Ambrosius, who is thought to have been responsible for the great linear earthwork,

Part of the immense stone circle at Avebury that lies inside Britain's largest henge monument.

Wansdyke which was 50 miles long, and part of which crosses the walk at Morgan's Hill, following the alignment of the earlier Roman road. Dates are imprecise, but by the end of the 6th century, the first kingdom of Wessex had been established on the coast and soon extended into what is now Wiltshire. The petty kings quarrelled amongst themselves, but by the 8th century the house of Mercia was established as the dominant force and even powerful Wessex formally recognised the protection of the ruler, Offa. It was a short-lived subservience.

After Offa's death, Wessex reclaimed its independence, and under Egbert went further, establishing overlordship over much of England – even Northumbria accepted his supremacy. Then, in AD 865, a new threat appeared as the 'Great Army' of the Danes landed in East Anglia and began to advance westward. At first the Wessex forces stood firm and under Aethelred and Alfred beat the Danes off in a battle on the Berkshire Downs. The success was temporary. Aethelred died and his brother Alfred was driven back into Somerset. There he regathered his forces, drove the Danes out of Wessex and earned himself the title, Alfred the Great. One reminder of Alfred's victories is the Westbury white horse. The original 9th century white horse was replaced in 1788, and the new one was modelled facing in the opposite direction.

Wessex was now at peace, and Alfred set about many improvements, including the establishment of *burhs* or fortified towns throughout the kingdom. Defence was not the only preoccupation, and a number of minsters were built, now often only remembered in place names such as Iwerne Minster and Beaminster, though even today it is notable that a modest place like Beaminster controls a very large parish. The most important ecclesiastical establishment of the Saxon period to be met along the Way is at Cerne Abbas. There are still traces of the abbey, including the magnificent porch to the abbot's house, but all the remains are medieval, nothing of the original Saxon foundation has survived.

The success of Alfred in gaining supremacy for Wessex was upheld well into the 10th century, when new Viking invaders threatened the peace. Wessex was then under the control of Aethelred the Unready – a name which has nothing to do with 'unready' as we know it, but comes from the Anglo-Saxon 'Unraed' or 'No Counsel'. He did, however, prove himself unready to cope with the Vikings and fled to Normandy. It marked the end of independent Wessex which under Cnut became part of the greater kingdom of England.

LITERARY WESSEX

The Wiltshire Downs seem to have attracted little attention from writers: Stonehenge is described by many, Avebury scarcely at all. One writer, otherwise almost unknown, provided a memorable image of the weathered shepherds in their landscape. George Ferebe wrote a Shepherd's Song for Queen Anne who visited the area in 1613, which ended with these lines:

> *Our comfort is, thy Greatness knows*
> *swarth faces, coarse cloth gowns,*
> *Are ornaments that well become*
> *the wide, wild, houseless downs.*

Dorset, in contrast, teems with literary associations, and there were few more passionate advocates of 'wide, wild' scenery than William and Dorothy Wordsworth. From September 1795 until July 1797 they lived at Racedown Lodge near Birdsmoorgate. From here a favourite walk was up Pilsden Pen. In her diary Dorothy described the views from a summit topped by stunted trees that 'suffered from the sea-blasts' out to 'the sea seen through different openings of the unequal hills', and nothing has changed much in the last two hundred years. It was here that Wordsworth, encouraged by his sister, seems to have first found his true voice.

> *She, in the midst of all, preserv'd me still*
> *A Poet, made me seek beneath that name*
> *My office upon earth, and nowhere else.*

It was here too that Coleridge bounded into their lives on his first visit, leaving the road by leaping a gate and striding to the house across the fields. He took them away to his cottage in the Quantocks, and there they stayed.

Leaping over gates seems normal behaviour for Coleridge, but anything so indecorous could only lead to a disaster in a Jane Austen novel. In *Persuasion*, a key scene involves a girl jumping down the steps of The Cobb at Lyme Regis.

> He advised her against it, thought the jar too great; but
> no, he reasoned and talked in vain; she smiled and said, 'I
> am determined I will': he put out his hands; she was too
> precipitate by half a second, she fell on the pavement of the
> Lower Cobb, and was taken up lifeless!

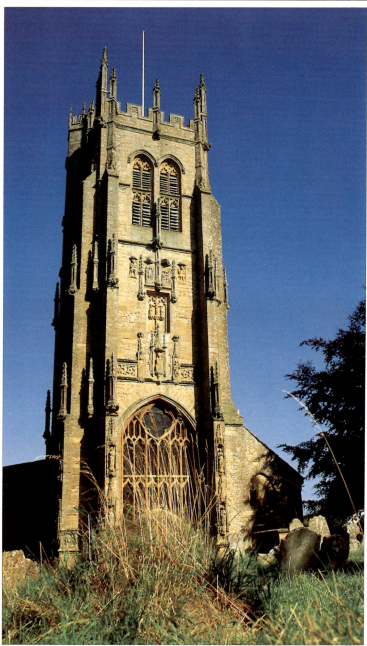

The church tower at Cerne Abbas, Abbot's Cernel as it appears in Hardy's Wessex, with its fine array of pinnacles and carved figures.

The girl recovered, but everyone in the novel found their lives changed. In John Fowles' twentieth century novel, The Cobb appears again, this time as the meeting place of the hero and the 'French Lieutenant's Woman'. Other scenes take place along the cliffs around Lyme.

The writer most famously associated with Wessex is Thomas Hardy, born at Upper Bockhampton, near Dorchester, in 1840. Not many of the places met along the Wessex Ridgeway feature in his works, though Cerne Abbas appears as Abbot's Cernel and Beaminster as Emminster, the latter probably closer in atmosphere to a country town of Hardy's day than any other. And this description from *Return of the Native* would fit any downland track.

> The long, laborious road, dry, empty, and white. It was quite open to the heath on each side, and bisected that vast dark surface like the parting-line on a head of black hair.

Where Hardy tends to conjure up visions of open heaths and wide landscapes, Geoffrey Household introduces a more secret Dorset of dark woods, hedgerows and hidden valleys. In *Rogue Male*, the hero hid from the assassin in the countryside near Sydling St Nicholas.

One author deserves special mention, though he is little known these days outside his native Dorset. William Barnes (1801–86) wrote his verse in local dialect. One of his best known poems is Linden Lea, but this verse should have a special appeal to walkers on the Wessex Ridgeway.

> *The zwellen downs, wi' chalky tracks*
> *A-climmen up their zunny backs,*
> *Do hide green meads an' zedgy brooks,*
> *An' clumps o' trees wi' glossy rooks,*
> *An' hearty vo'k to laugh an' zing,*
> *An' parish-churches in a string,*
> *Wi' tow'rs o' merry bells to ring,*
> *An' white roads up athirt the hills.*

GEOLOGY AND SCENERY

The dominant theme of the landscape through which this walk passes is chalk. Look at a geological map of England and the chalk areas take the form of some strange beast. The fat body squats over Salisbury Plain: one limb heads north towards The Wash; two others head south east as the North and South Downs, while the other goes off to the south west and the Dorset coast. It is this latter arm that the Wessex Ridgeway follows for the greater part of the route, mainly staying close to the edge where the downland dips away towards the valleys.

Scenery is a long time forming. Some 500 million years ago, a platform of hard rock covered the whole region. In time, it sank and rivers and watercourses brought down deposits; the heaviest settling as clays with what is now the greensand layer above that. In the Cretaceous period that began around 150 million years ago, the area was entirely covered by water, home to a myriad of tiny creatures.

As they died, their shells and skeletons fell to the ocean floor where they were pressed together to form chalk. It built up steadily over another hundred million years until great upheavals in the earth's crust thrust up the high mountains of The Alps and pushed the chalk above water to form a great dome which stretched all the way across what is now southern England to northern France. Over succeeding aeons the chalk weathered. The sea broke through to create the English Channel and wind and rain eroded the dome. The centre collapsed down to the underlying clays, while rivers and streams created the valleys. These were the processes that created the typical landscape of the downs. Where the dome fractured, steep scarp faces were formed. At the edges, it weathered more gently to create smooth rounded hills. Beyond in the lowlands there is a narrow band of greensand, and outside that the heavier clays.

It is difficult to grasp the immense age of the landscape, and even more difficult to imagine what its earliest inhabitants might have been. However, Lyme Regis at the end of the walk is famous for its fossils. The most common are the ammonites, sea creatures that lived as long ago as 200 million years, whose spiral shells can be up to 2 metres in diameter. Other fossils which the diligent might still find are the less spectacular belemnites. No one nowadays is likely to enjoy the success of the first great collector in the area, Mary Anning, who uncovered an ichthyosaur in 1811, followed that with a plesiosaur and had her greatest moment when she discovered a superb example of a pterodactyl. If there is much along the way that gives a sense of history, there is not much against which to measure the scale of geological time. If one took the period from the first laying down of the chalk to the present as a 'geological year', then the whole kingdom of Wessex was only in existence for less than a minute: it is quite a thought to take on a walk.

The end of the walk in sight: a view of the sea from Coney's Castle.

THE FARMING LANDSCAPE

The earliest evidence of farming activity is found in the upland regions. This is not surprising since the earliest form of plough, perhaps consisting of no more than a forked tree branch, the ends reinforced by stone axe-heads, could make little impression on heavy soils, but would be adequate for the lighter soils of the hills. Excavation under a barrow near Avebury revealed a criss-cross pattern of plough marks made in Neolithic times. Walkers can have no idea of what this primitive farming landscape would have been like, for there is no visible evidence in the landscape we see today. But by the end of the Bronze Age around 700 BC, farmers were cultivating fields, divided by low banks or lynchets. A whole set of small, square fields can easily be identified just south of the Way on Fyfield Down. One other ancient settlement crops up along the route at Ringmoor. This one dates back to the Roman occupation, and here there are traces of the old farm tracks as well as the ghostly outlines of fields. Does this mean that only the uplands were farmed? Not necessarily, rather that over the centuries as ploughing methods improved, with plough shares that could turn sods instead of just scratch the surface, crop growing became concentrated in the valleys. From those centuries all traces of any prehistoric systems would have been largely obliterated.

Most of the field system we see today has developed out of the enclosure system begun in Tudor times and continued through the 17th and 18th centuries. This is the familiar pattern of squared fields, divided by fence, hedgerow and wall. But in places, some of the medieval pattern of open fields divided up into strips has survived. There are many points along the way where the hillside looks as if it has been turned into a great staircase, with a series of flat ledges cut into the slope. These are known as 'strip lynchets' and are no more than the medieval cultivation strips extended up the slope. Some of the best examples can be seen along the edge of Salisbury Plain between Market Lavington and Bratton.

A good deal of the walk, as its name suggests, keeps to the high land of the downs, which is traditionally open land where sheep graze. Although many farms had fields of crops in the valley, the flocks were seen as the mainstay of the business. The shepherd of the 19th century was regarded as the aristocrat of farm workers. Life was hard, and in the lambing season shepherds stayed out on the hills for weeks on end, living in portable huts. They were justifiably proud of their skills. A popular legend at Bratton tells how one shepherd,

Frank Whatley, won a wager when his dog rounded up twenty sheep and got them all standing in the eye of the White Horse.

Today, patterns are changing: small fields are amalgamated into ever larger units, while more and more upland areas go under the plough. Enough of the past remains, however, to give the walker a glimpse into farming history stretching back over thousands of years.

Farming old and new: tractor wheels leave a regular pattern across a modern field of grain, while cattle graze on medieval strip lynchets.

THE
WESSEX
RIDGEWAY

1 Marlborough to Devizes

via Avebury   *16½ miles (27 km)*

Marlborough **1** is a town with an air of comfortable self satisfaction, not exactly smug but certainly pleased with its own elegant urbanity – and with a good deal of justification. Situated on the River Kennet at a point which has been at a major road crossing since Roman times, it was a natural market centre for the region. The broad high street with its many inns establishes the character immediately, but it was a series of accidents that resulted in a very satisfying unity and a wealth of good, unpretentious Georgian building. In the 17th century there were a number of serious fires – after the last of which the authorities banished thatch for ever from the town centre – and it is the rebuilding after the fires that gives Marlborough its tone.

At the southern end of the main street is the now redundant church of St Peter and St Paul. To reach the start of the walk, go up the street from the church and turn left down Hyde Lane next to the

A gloriously rich mix of buildings in the centre of Marlborough.

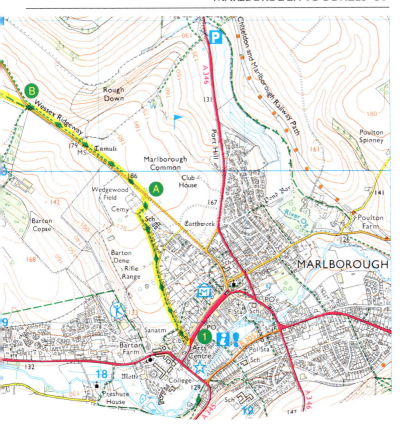

library. On reaching the tennis courts and playing fields take the path along the side of the fields beside the road. Carry on beside rough-surfaced Leaze Road, and where that ends continue on past the gates to the old cemetery. Follow this round to the right, between the old and new graveyards, to reach the road **A** and turn left. The view at once opens out to the sort of scenery that will dominate much of the way, a gentle green swell of hills that roll off into the distance. The road itself with its broad grass verges and formal avenue of trees seems altogether too grand for its present modest status, and the presence of an old milestone adds confirmation. This was, in fact, at one time the main road to Bath. The route continues past the golf course which occupies part of the old Marlborough Common.

Where the road turns right by the entrance to Manton House Farm **B** carry straight on along the bridleway signposted to Avebury. It is perhaps more surprising to find that this rough track is also on the line of the old main road. Racehorse gallops align with the track – and walkers who want to measure their own speeds can time themselves by the furlong posts. Soon the sound of the traffic recedes to be replaced by the welcoming song of the skylark. Numbers are sadly decreasing and it is impossible to imagine a downland walk without this melodic accompaniment. All the while the views seem to get larger and wider as the walk stretches out along the ridge leading away from Marlborough. The gallops end by a long line of firs, but the track carries straight on, and as the prospect opens up over delightful scenery of open country it becomes clear what a natural, dry, high-level walk this is, a major route as far back as Saxon times when it was a herepath or military road. Down to the left are the extensive buildings of Manton House and, in spite of the thin chalky soil, scattered with flints, there are extensive patches of arable fields climbing the hillside.

Where the path divides by a clump of tall beech trees **C** – a landscape feature that will seem like an old friend by the end of the walk – take the track to the left signposted to Avebury. The long, gentle climb from Marlborough ends at a reservoir in front of a conifer plantation. The landscape is patched with woodland and the solitary song of the lark is drowned out by the more raucous lads of the bird band, cantankerous

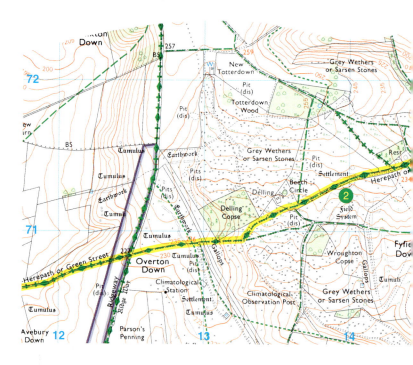

rooks and harsh-voiced pheasants. A number of paths cross the Way, but the route keeps heading steadily forwards. The scenery which has been grand all the way, just keeps on getting grander, and now there is an immense prospect of hills, their contours emphasized by lines of trees that roll with the hills, like foam on the crests of waves. The track then enters the Fyfield Down National Nature Reserve, where the hillside is dotted with massive sarsen stones, which in the distant view do resemble a flock of grazing sheep, hence their other name of 'grey weathers'. They support a rich variety of lichens, and an expert could no doubt identify them all, but even to an untutored eye they offer an amazing variety of colours and textures, from silvery grey to violent orange.

Over to the left **2** a series of low ridges defines the boundaries of an ancient field system, popularly known as 'Celtic fields', then the track dips down to a hollow with a straggle of thorn trees and a little, abandoned tile-hung farmhouse. Gorse bushes provide cover for a lively rabbit population, and the path swings above the end of a dry valley before climbing back up the hill. At the top use two gates to cross the gallops and then take the right hand of two metal gates. Turn half right away from the fence and the clear path is abandoned for a pleasant walk across the turf with the distant Cherhill monument providing a useful marker.

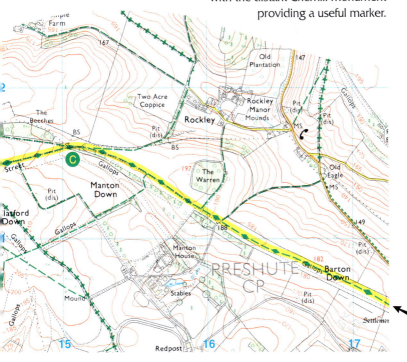

At the gate by the signpost, the Wessex Ridgeway crosses the other Ridgeway, and becomes a rutted track heading downhill towards Avebury, and soon the banks of the great henge come into view. At Manor Farm, the track gives way to a metalled road that passes through the bank **3** to reach Avebury itself, sitting in the centre of the ring. It is impossible to pass by without spending time among the massive sarsen stones and for those who want to explore the archaeological sites of the region, a circular walk can be taken from here (p.48). (Please note that numbered points of interest 3 – 6 appear on this walk.) The Way continues through the village, where there is more to explore, including museums and the manor house (NT). The route goes down the High Street, marked as a dead end, passing Manor Farm with its unusual Dutch gables and on to the church. This is well worth a visit, a typical hotchpotch begun by the Saxons and altered by everyone else up to the Victorians. The Norman font is truly remarkable and features an understandably nervous looking bishop, who seems to be wearing his party frock, trying to keep a terrifying dragon at bay with his crozier.

A broad track follows the line of racehorse gallops on the downs above Marlborough.

Follow the road round to the right, past ambling peacocks, passing the end of the churchyard, and then left to cross a stream with a view of the astonishing cone of Silbury Hill. Once over the stream **D** take the path to the left. Go through a wooden gate into the field and take the path beside the fence. Cross a stile to join the rough road in front of the houses. Continue on the path in front of the bungalows and follow it round to the left to a T-junction and turn right down the road.

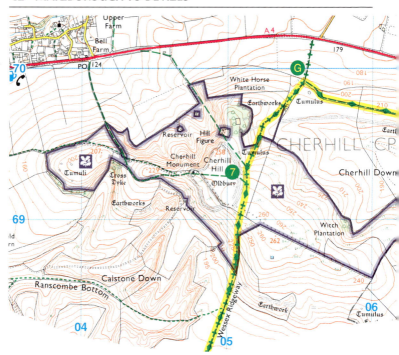

The houses are soon left behind, and the Way goes through a very different landscape of flat fields of grain. There are still memories of the distant past: to the right is Windmill Hill with its earthworks and burial mounds, and there are two massive standing stones near the path which have seemingly wandered over from the henge. Where the road sweeps left by the buildings continue straight on along the track and where that divides **E** turn left down the tree-lined green path. This is still very much horse country where walkers are liable to meet strings of thoroughbreds on their way to the gallops.

Turn right at the main road, keeping on the pavement until reaching a very handsome milestone **F**, then cross to the lay-by and take the path that leaves the road at the far end, heading towards the clump of trees. Although the modern road has been left behind, the Way is still running on the older Bath road. The flat plain to the north, however, is abandoned as the route returns to the springy turf and the long straight lines of the gallops. Leaving the fine stand of beech behind, an obvious track leads down to a long ridge above earthworks which offers superb views out over miles of countryside to the south, with no more than a few scattered farms to interrupt the broad sweep of the landscape. The path is very much part of a physical

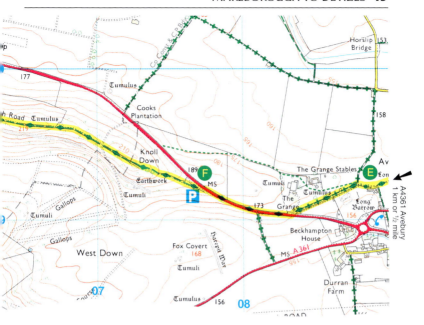

boundary between the flat land with its fields of crops and the rougher downland. Eventually the track becomes closed in between fences, with high banks that limit the view – though the monument continues to provide an unmissable waymark.

The track divides by a round barrow, a Bronze Age burial mound **G**. Turn left onto the chalky track heading uphill. At a barn, take the path to the right, and go through the metal gate heading towards the obvious gap in the ramparts of Oldbury Hill Fort **7**. Although the track runs along the bottom of the ramparts, it is certainly tempting to explore this, the first of many Iron Age forts to be met along the Way. It has typical defences of double banks and ditches, and a turned entrance to make a direct assault more difficult. From the top of the hill, crowned with its 19th century obelisk, there are fine views – a peep over the hillside to the north reveals an 18th century white horse.

Returning to the Way, follow the line of the ramparts, with a wire fence to the left. It emerges to an area of turf with no clear path, but the next objective soon appears in the form of a gate in the fence ahead, beyond which a more definite path winds downhill through scrub. The view opens out over a billowing landscape of contrasting shades, with the rich green of the slopes breaking into a rusty brown as the land slides away into clefts and hollows. The path straightens out and heads directly downhill to reach a broad track, running along the course of an old Roman road in the valley bottom. Go *through* the gate **H** and turn right onto the track at the field's edge. This is very peaceful countryside, which provides ample opportunity to see and hear the local wildlife – which, in Spring, could well include a hare 'boxing match' or a partridge erupting from the corn in a noisy flurry. Round barrows heave up above fields of crops, and there are views back to the hill fort. The way goes slowly but steadily uphill and all the time the view widens, and radio masts appear up ahead, marking the summit. Eventually the track runs beside the Wiltshire Trust Nature Reserve, an area of rough grassland, while to the right a steep wooden hillside slips away to a grassy hollow. This section is deeply rutted, so it comes as some relief when, at the far side of the wood **I**, a gate gives access to a path through the nature reserve. It swings away to the left and curves up the hill, spotted with an acne-like eruption of mole hills.

At the top of the hill **8** the path passes through the great Anglo-Saxon earthwork of Wansdyke by a marker post to arrive, rather surprisingly, at the neat greens and fairways of a golf course. Keep to the left hand side of the course as far as the track that turns right towards the clubhouse. Cross the road, and take the wide track to the left of the buildings. This is a byway used by vehicles, but fortunately wide

Lichen covered stones dot the landscape of Fyfield Down, and are known as 'grey wethers'.

6 km or 3½ miles
A361 Devizes

enough to allow room for walking in comfort. We are now back to the large fields and flatlands of the plain – and a place where the Royalists, following the road out of Marlborough, met the Parliamentary forces in battle in 1643. Where tracks cross in the hollow **J** turn right onto the bridleway. This becomes a surfaced road, and at the junction by the house with Gothic windows **K**, take the road to the left. The level uniformity ends to the right where the land falls away in folds and convolutions. At the next track junction continue straight on to the summit of the little hill **L**, then turn sharp left to follow the edge above the ever more twisted and steep slope, up to the ramparts of the little triangular hill fort, Oliver's Castle. At the end of the earthworks turn left along the escarpment edge to reach a car parking area **M**. At the time the path was walked the official Way was inaccessible and this description is of the route actually followed. Both are shown on the map.

Turn right onto the straight track which joins a road that begins to turn downhill. At a metal gate **N** cross the stile to take the path heading directly and steeply downwards beside what is now a great rarity, a recently planted hedge. Cross a stile at the foot of the hill, go down a small dip and then follow the fence to cross a second stile to join the road. Turn left on the road and as soon as the next corner is turned, take the footpath on the right by the house. By the house entrance turn right to take the obvious path across the field towards the houses. Cross straight over the road and take the long, straight track opposite, which heads down a formal avenue of trees. This is Quaker's Walk, originally the grand approach to Roundway House, home of the wealthy Colston family. It ends at ornate iron gates, beyond which is the Kennet and Avon Canal. The walk at this point crosses the bridge and turns left onto the towpath. Those who want to explore the town, to hunt out refreshment or a bed for the night should continue straight on into Devizes.

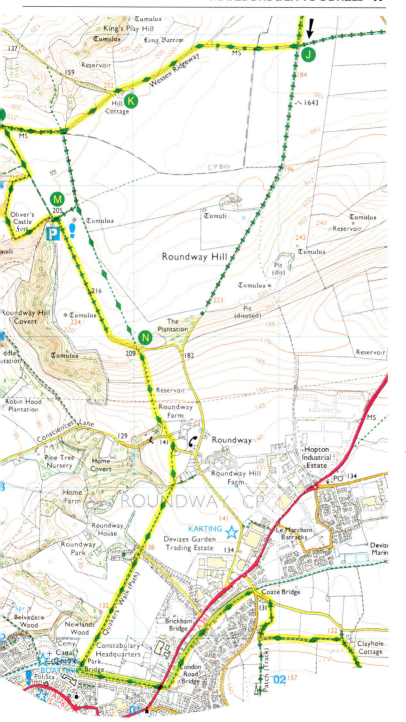

CIRCULAR WALK FROM AVEBURY

5 miles (8.5 km)

This walk takes in all the more important archaeological sites in the Avebury area, a fuller description of which can be found on p.00. From the centre of Avebury village **A** retrace your steps along the Wessex Ridgeway for approximately half a mile, leaving the henge circle to pass the buildings of Manor Farm. At the end of the barns, where ways cross **B**, turn right on the byway, signposted to Overton Hill and Bath Road. The walk now continues over very open country, broken by occasional clumps of trees and soon the rough way gives way to a more pleasant grassy track. As it begins to climb the view opens out on the right to the stone avenue that forms a processional way linking Avebury henge to The Sanctuary. As the track approaches the nearer clump of trees, they can be seen to stand on the remains of round barrows.

The track swings left to a junction with the Ridgeway long distance path **C**. Turn right and continue on down towards the A4 which lies just beyond the imposing group of round barrows in the field on the left. Over to the right, the top of Silbury Hill can be seen, poking above the fields. Cross straight over the main road to take the track opposite. Immediately to the right is the site of The Sanctuary **4**, which began as a wooden shrine, later replaced by stone circles, whose position is indicated by concrete posts. Continue down the path with The Sanctuary on the right, passing another large round barrow on the left. This is a more intimate landscape than that of the downland, with small fields divided by hedgerows and villages spread out along the little valley – West Overton to the left with an imposing church tower, East Kennet straight ahead with a more modest steeple. The path heads downhill, but just before it turns left to a byway sign by a bridge, turn right through a metal gate **D**. The path runs beside a stream, with a view across to an elegant house, with a gazebo in the wall.

On reaching the road **E** turn left to cross the bridge, then immediately right beyond the little pumping station. Where tracks join, carry straight on for about 10 metres, then turn right onto the path running between tall hawthorn hedges. At the end of this short section cross a stile and turn left keeping to the line of the fence. Cross over the roadway and continue on the track opposite, along the edge of the field. West Kennet long barrow appears in silhouette on the left and Silbury

Hill rises in its full splendour up ahead. At the path junction **F**, turn left to visit the long barrow **5**, a diversion well worth making, for this is one of the most impressive burial sites in England, with immense slabs at the entrance and forming the roof. Return down the path and continue on to the main road. Cross straight over and go through the gate opposite the lay-by. The path signposted to Avebury runs up beside the stream through a series of gates and over stiles, affording a splendid opportunity to see Silbury Hill **6** at close quarters.

Turn right at the road **G** then immediately left into the National Trust car park. Take the path from the diagonally opposite corner that leads back into the village.

Scale is approx 2¼ inches to 1 mile

The view south from the walk, looking across the convoluted landscape of Calstone Do

2 DEVIZES TO WEST LAVINGTON

via Urchfont

10 miles (16 km)

The first part of this section of the Way uses the towpath of the Kennet and Avon Canal which was begun in 1793 under the direction of the engineer John Rennie. It runs from Bath in the west, where the navigable Avon leads on through Bristol to the sea, to Newbury in the east, and via the River Kennet to the Thames and London. The artificial nature of the waterway is immediately apparent as it runs through a deep cutting, providing an isolated green way through the town, where coot and mallard are more in evidence than cars and trucks. It passes under a particularly handsome road bridge, built of local stone with keystone and string course emphasized as restrained decoration. The canal now swings left past houses, many of which have boats at the ends of their gardens: it is hard now to believe that just a few years ago all this was derelict, a mere muddy ditch. Continue under the next bridge to a modern replacement, perfectly decent and lined out in blue engineering bricks **A**. It is here that the Way leaves the canal.

Narrow boats on the Kennet & Avon Canal, Devizes.

Take the path up to the road, cross straight over and take the road opposite, signposted to Coate. Turn almost immediately right onto the green track. At the top of a short climb as the track swings back towards the houses **B**, turn left along the footpath marked 'Public Footpath No Horses' – along which, interestingly, there were a good many more hoof-prints than footprints! The narrow path runs between high hedges sepa-rating it from the surrounding farmland. As it ends, a broad green track takes over, climbing a gentle slope, from the top of which the view once again opens out to downland, its arrival confirmed by the return of the skylark's song. The track winds on towards the hills but for the time being it stays with the valley floor with its immense fields which are more rem-iniscent of East Anglia than Wessex. The route goes straight forward at the track-crossing and then climbs over modest Etchilhampton Hill and drops down the other side again. Cross straight over the minor road, and take the track opposite, which soon begins to swing away to the left between wire fences. Where tracks cross continue straight on down a little tree-shaded path, whose branches meet overhead to create a green tunnel, that leads down to the main road **C**.

Cross straight over the road and take the minor road, signposted to Stert. Once in the village turn left on the road signposted to Fullaway Farm. This is a typical West Country lane, sunk down between high banks speckled with flowers and topped by trees. It passes through the abutments of what was once a bridge on the railway line to Devizes, one of the many to fall to Dr Beeching's axe. The road arrives at a neat farm with a duck pond complete with resident ducks, and the view opens out to the village of Stert straggling out along the ridge, with a little church rising above a slightly curious bow-fronted house. This is a delightful stretch of country, full of secretive dips and hollows, wholly rural – apart from a distant tall chimney which will be a companion in view for many miles. The road twists and turns to give a constantly changing viewpoint of woods and fields, birds sing in the woods and rabbits lollop in the fields. The distant view rolls away with a sparse spattering of farms and hamlets, a true rural idyll.

Go through a metal gate, but do not take the obvious track signposted to the watermill. Stay by the hedge on the left and, past the cattle grid, turn left through a gate on the left **D**, heading straight across the field to the posts opposite and a gap in the hedge. Beyond the next gateway, turn half left towards the stile at the edge of the woods. Take the obvious path through the trees to wooden steps which lead up to the railway **9**, the main line West Country route through Castle Cary, once part of the great GWR empire. It was originally built to the broad gauge of 7ft between the rails, and when these were removed in the 1890s and replaced by standard gauge, parts of the old track proved quite useful. Cross over the line and you can see some of the old cut-down rails still serving as fence posts.

Cross the stile and continue on the path which runs at a slight angle from the fence to cross two stiles and reach a footbridge over a stream. Continue alongside the stream to join a farm track that comes in from the left and follow it round as it turns off to the right. The next immediate objective, Urchfont church tower, now appears in view and the track turns towards it. Once round the corner, cross the stile **E** in the fence and continue across the field with the fence on the right to a footbridge and stile and climb the hill towards the farm buildings. At the far right corner of the field, cross the farm track to a stile and continue beside the fence to join the houses by the road at the edge of Urchfont **10**. This is an attractive spot with a mixture of old buildings using both brick and timber framing.

At the road, turn right then immediately left. Turn left at a little triangular green, and the road swings past a pond, and is followed past the Nag's Head to reach the B-road. Turn right down the B-road and as it begins to swing right, cross to a triangular parking area **F** and turn down the trackway between the houses.

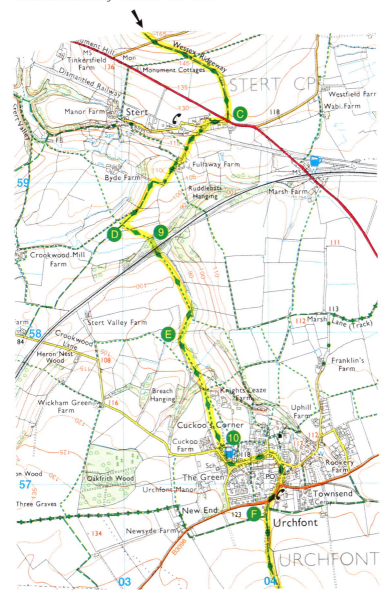

This is a sunken path which goes steadily uphill and for a time the only wide view you can get is by looking back. All that changes when the path emerges into the light. Now there is a splendid panorama, looking back to the long, low ripple of hills over which the Way has already passed to another long row of hills up ahead, with a promise of still more climbs to come. Soon the path begins to dive deep into the hillside, cut right down to the hard chalk. The sweet sounds of lark

Poppies, daisies, meadow vetchling and a colourful variety of grasses brighten meadows at the edge of the downs.

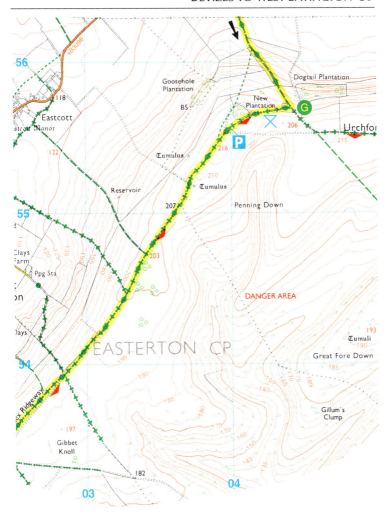

and yellowhammer are likely to be joined by the thudding explosions or sharp outbursts of rattling bangs, for the route is about to reach the edge of the Westdown Artillery Range.

At the top of the hill by a dew pond **G**, turn right onto the broad gravel track heading towards a clump of beech trees. Once through the trees, the ridgeway walk really lives up to its name, with superb views to either side. To the right one can look across the valley with its pattern of regular fields and villages all the way across to the downs where the Cherhill monument is still a prominent feature. To the left is a seemingly empty landscape, the vast expanse of Salisbury Plain.

This looks on the map to be simply a boring, straight line trudge – which it would easily become in bad weather – but when the sun shines and the air is clear it is pure delight. On reaching the access road to the range, the gravel gives way to tarmac, and beyond a large flagpole it begins to head back downhill. At the end of the next large field on the right **H** opposite the farm access road, turn right onto the track that soon begins to steepen as it heads towards the valley floor. It cuts through a small wood and then leaves the more obvious road, heading slightly away to the right. At the end of the strip of trees look over to the right to see the array of terraces cut into the hillside **11**. These are medieval strip lynchets or cultivation terraces, the hillside equivalent of the strips of open fields in the valley. Here turn left **I** onto the path and continue on to the road beyond the thatched cottage to reach the main road and the village of West Lavington **12**.

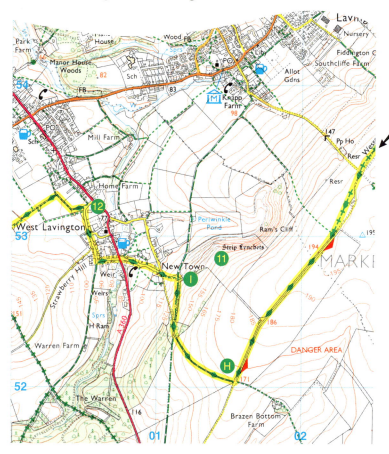

Dial House, West Lavington: the derivation of the name is obvious when one looks above the front door.

3 WEST LAVINGTON TO HEYTESBURY

via Warminster   *18½ miles (31 km)*

The minor road reaches the A360 at Dial House, aptly named as it boasts a particularly grand sundial over the main door. Cross the road and the stream on the far side, with its beautiful clear water. It may not seem a significant feature today, but in the past it was this more than anything that led to the village growing up at just this spot, even if it now supports nothing more than a few mallard. Carry on up Rickbarton, and at the top of this steep little hill, turn right into White Street. The route passes close by the surprisingly grand church, with its overflow graveyard reached by a bridge across a sunken lane. The church itself is notable for its elaborate memorials, including the Danvers monument, showing the 21 year old who died in 1654, leaning languid and sorrowful as if modelling for the image of a romantic poet. The church itself has seen so many additions through the centuries that it is as difficult to make sense of the plan from the interior as it is from the outside.

The melancholy Danvers memorial in West Lavington church.

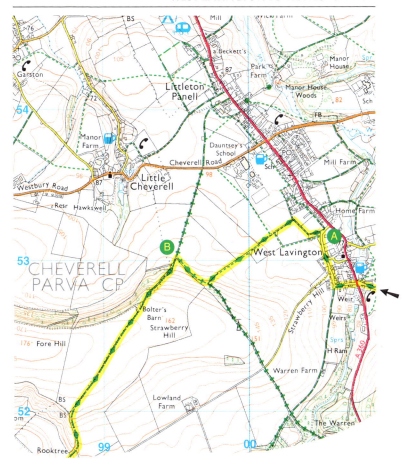

Where the road begins to turn right towards an ornate gateway **A**, turn left onto the footpath to go through a kissing gate to follow the path that turns right by a hawthorn hedge. Beyond the next gate turn left up the path between the trees, with a sports complex over to the right. Emerging from the hedges, the path runs beside a fence through some farmland, and there is a good view back over the village to the strip lynchets striping the hillside. There is now a steady climb up towards a strip of woodland where the path turns right. At the track junction **B** turn left up the path that runs towards woodland. The path leads through a thicket, tangled with bramble, and climbs past an area where, at the fringe, the dominant species is birch instead of the ubiquitous beech. At the end of the wood, where the track divides, carry straight on and by the time you reach the top of the hill you are very

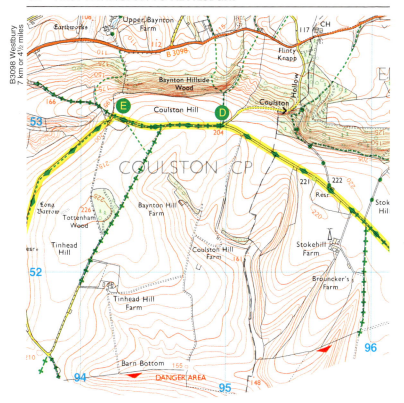

much back with the upland and its vistas. This is a pleasant green track with a newly planted line of trees, which dips briefly to pass round below a small copse. It is a short respite, for there is now all too clear a climb to the top of the escarpment **C**.

The walk has arrived at The Imber Range Perimeter Path, which will be a familiar feature for many miles. Turn right along a track very similar to the one met earlier. On the plain there are signs of old field systems and boundaries, but wide areas are comparatively featureless apart from the occasional straggling, woebegone hedge. This is more than compensated for by the views out over the valley, where little villages are strung out along the ribbon of the road. On reaching the farm approach, the track gives way to a surfaced road, and the landscape becomes more varied. Woodland spreads up the hillside, and the land to the south suddenly starts swooping and diving in a succession of hillocks and hollows. At the junction **D** where the road swings back on itself, continue straight on along the broad, rough track, now running through a mixture of arable fields and rough grassland. Where this wide way swings left, carry straight on along the somewhat narrower track with a row of trees alongside. Again, this follows the route of the old turnpike road, this time from Bath to Salisbury – or Sarum as it says on the milestone dated 1757 beside the track.

Coming down the hill, the path divides again **E**. Turn left off the byway onto a footpath. Go to the left of the little wooded hollow and look for a stile on the right with a waymarker on it. Once across the stile take the path at the edge of the field with a fence on the right and a view down over a deep, wooded hollow. The tall chimney which was first noted back at Stert puts in an appearance, but is now a great deal closer. Looking at the contortions of the landscape below the scarp edge, one can scarcely imagine the natural forces that could take a landmass such as this and squeeze and crumple it like a paper ball. Down in the gap, there is a glimpse of the village of Edington.

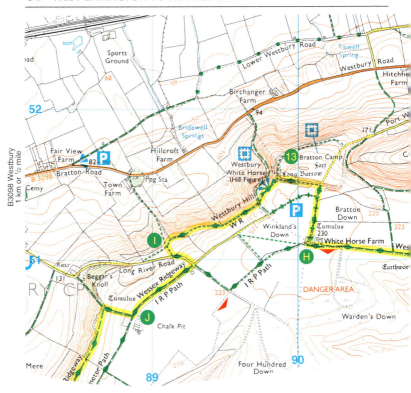

The track bends sharply right and heads steeply downhill to join the road. Turn right, then immediately left onto the farm track heading up to the barns **F**. Once past them, take the track on the left, a pleasant green lane running through farmland. It eventually arrives at a hilltop road **G**. Turn right, then left at the next junction to rejoin the perimeter road. This goes steadily uphill, and the route is much like the previous section, with the wide views over the populous valley on one side, and the empty land of dips and folds on the other: a delight in the sun, this can be an unnervingly desolate section in bad weather, with no protection as the few patches of trees roar back at the wind. The walk does now finally reach the tall chimney, part of a large cement works just outside Westbury.

At the farm buildings where the track divides **H** continue on just past the junction to cross a stile on the right for a pleasant walk across the turf to the obvious ramparts of the hill fort, Bratton Camp **13**. When first seen from across the down it seems a disappointing, insignificant affair, with low earthworks, but once the first line of ram-

parts is reached, the land falls away in a very deep ditch with a high bank on the other side. Altogether this is a very impressive site, with a long barrow thrown in for extra interest. From the end of the ramparts one can look down over Westbury and, more interestingly, the White Horse. This is the figure originally cut to celebrate Alfred the Great's victory over the Danes. From the ramparts turn left along the escarpment above the Horse where a panorama identifies the places of interest on view. There is a pleasant walk along the edge, where soil-creep has created a pattern of ripples, like those left by a retreating tide, running along the contours of the hillside.

Where woodland appears at the edge of the hill **I** turn left up the field towards a stile and then turn left up the road. At the top of the hill, turn right by the entrance to the chalk quarry. Once again we are back with the range path, this time running along the edge of the immense pit which provides the raw material for the cement works in the valley. The visit to the path is, however, a brief one. Where the track divides by a metal tower **J** turn right onto the bridleway. The track dips downhill, then where it divides, turn left through a wooden gate to take the path at the escarpment edge, looking down over

Westbury. This is as good a section of walking as any on the edge, combining a good footpath underfoot, an airy viewpoint and a splendid landscape, parcelled up by hedgerows sprouting mature trees at regular intervals. Reaching the woodland, the view may be lost but there is ample compensation in the magnificent, old beech trees that line the route. These give way to an area of coppice, and the section ends at a clearing **K**. Turn onto the bridleway that turns back at a sharp angle to the left. This runs back up the hill where there is a right turn to rejoin our old acquaintance, the perimeter path.

On rejoining the path, the focus of attention shifts to the land to the left of the Way, where little wooded hollows seem to offer the very model of rural peace – apart, of course, from the noise of artillery. Where the track gives way to a surfaced road **L** turn left over a stile to take the path in the field beside the fence. This swoops down to a hollow and climbs part of the way back up the other side to a line of trees. At the top of the field, cross the stile and turn left, then almost immediately right past a barn.

A stile with the Wessex Ridgeway waymark on the escarpment edge above Edington.

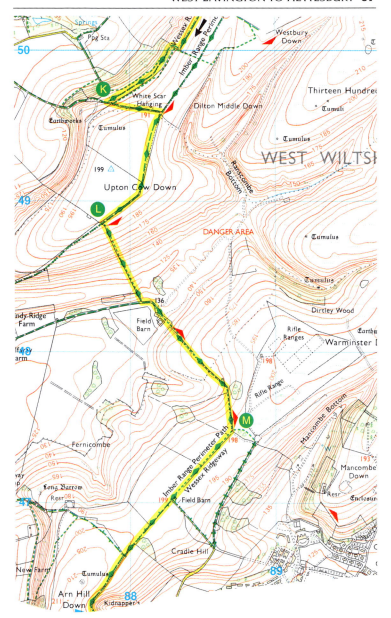

Nearing the top of the hill by a clump of trees **M**, turn right onto a wide grassy track that continues straight on along the top of the ridge past a field until it reaches the edge of the golf course. Continue on the same track, beside the fence, and there is now a fine view of the next hill fort.

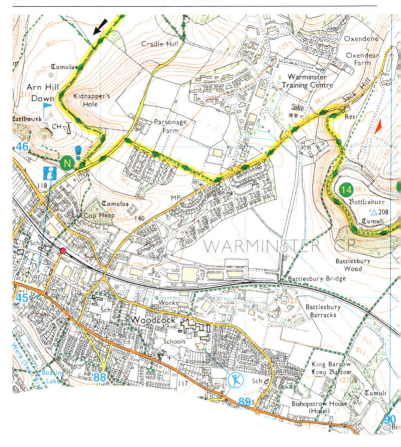

Keep to the fence as the track turns round the end of a deep, dry valley, where the rough, tufted hillside contrasts with the lush flat meadow in the valley floor, beyond which is the army camp.

Passing the clubhouse, the track begins to head downhill, and narrows to a footpath, which turns down towards the road **N**. Turn left along the road, and at the first road junction turn right past the formally paraded army houses. At the next road junction, turn left passing the camp. The road soon begins to climb, then near the top of the hill, turn right onto a footpath signposted, unsurprisingly, Imber Range Path, and a prospect of a trio of hills lies ahead. Follow the path round the edge of the field as it turns to head for the ramparts of Battlesbury hill fort **14**. This is as imposing as any met along the way, with hugely impressive earthworks – and it seems the defences were tested, for what is believed to be a war cemetery has been discovered by archaeologists nearby.

Follow the path round to the right along the outer ramparts, and one can see how the steep slopes and fortifications must have made it all but impregnable in its day, some 2,000 years ago. Continue on past the wood until a point is reached where the ramparts are all but level with the fields. Look out for a waymarked stile just below the earthworks **O**, cross it and follow the path going downhill towards two barns. The path now heads towards the next hill, this time distinguished by a great array of strip lynchets **15**, while more appear on the hillside to the left. The path soon climbs again. Head towards a gap in the hedge at the foot of the hill and now the path becomes indistinct. Turn half right to cross the shoulder of the hill, rounding it to pass above the patch of woodland on the right, then head downhill to the road junction **P**.

Carry straight on along the road for a few paces, and then turn right across the stile to head for the third hill and the next hill fort. Turn left on reaching the lower ramparts, and there is a good view back to the strip lynchets of Middle Hill. Continue following the fence, leaving the line of the fort and passing above a wooded hollow. Ignore all stiles until reaching one which has the Wessex Ridgeway mark and leads to a path heading across fields to a wood. Carry straight on through the wood, and at the far side turn right **Q**, leaving the Imber Range path for the very last time, and taking the path beside the trees. The village of Heytesbury comes into view, with its remarkably large church **16**. Follow the field edge and look out for a path on the right leading down to the main road. Cross straight over and take the path into the centre of Heytesbury.

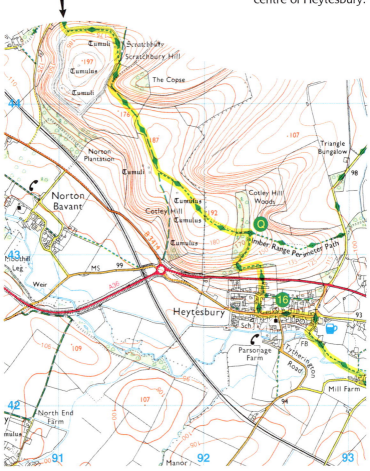

The Westbury white horse carved into the hillside beneath the ramparts of Bratton Camp.

4 Heytesbury to Ludwell

via Corton, Hindon and Wardour Castle   *17 miles (27.5 km)*

Turn left down the main village street, passing the tiny village lock-up with its conical roof: the locals were not expecting a major crime wave. At the far end turn right down the lane that leads to Mill Street and take the track to the left down to the river bank. It joins the river close to an attractive arched footbridge. Follow the river round to the left and where it wanders off on a long meander carry straight on across the field and rejoin the river where it returns by a former mill, a handsome, well-proportioned building. Go through a kissing gate by the mill to join the road by the bridge **A**. Turn right to cross the bridge and then right up the road, which then turns left to pass in front of the mill and immediately right. At this point turn left onto a green track, then a left and right dog-leg to join a footpath at the side of the field, with hedge and stream to the right. The path heads on a diagonal across the field and then returns to the river bank, close to the footbridge **B** which marks the start of a circular walk from Knook on the opposite bank (see p.84).

Cross a stile and turn right onto the path over the field and cross a footbridge. The path swings left and becomes a more definite route, running between hedges. It passes under the railway arch that carries the main line from Salisbury to Bath. At the far side it emerges at the village of Corton, passing an imaginative chapel conversion. At the road junction **C** turn left and stay on the road as it swings round to the right, passing a grand, thatched, stone house, Little Manor – which makes one wonder how much grander the big manor might be. Just before reaching the triangular green turn left up a bridleway, cross the road and continue straight on along the path opposite. The narrow path, worn down to the underlying chalk, climbs steadily, shut in by hedges to either side. Arriving at a roadway **D** turn left through a procession of tall beech on a long but gentle climb. At the barns where ways divide **E** leave the surfaced road for the rough track on the right, and where this ends, continue straight on along the green path that heads for the woodland spread out along the horizon. There is just time to savour the rolling farmland before the woods close in. The woodland, however, has its own delights to offer which provide more than adequate compensation.

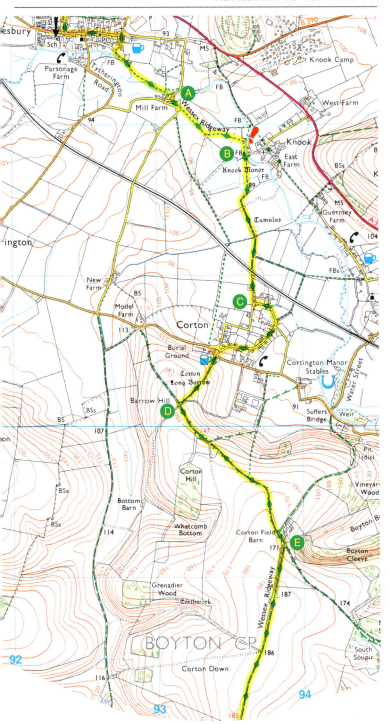

This curious little building in Heytesbury was once the village lock-up, where local drunks could be left to wait for a sober awakening.

At first, there is mixed woodland to one side, conifer to the other, but soon the latter comes to dominate. The path swings round to the right by a triangular clearing, and the way is brightened by great banks of rhododendra. This is an attractive wood, not as densely planted as many, and there is a very good chance of seeing deer either here in the wood itself or nipping out for a browse in the fields. At a large clearing **F** look out for a direction post and turn left onto the path through the trees. Go over one crossing and at the next **G** turn right by a Wessex Ridgeway marker and follow the path round to the left and continue on round the edge of the wood. Where the trees end, take the obvious path down to the busy main road.

Cross straight over onto the track opposite for a long steady climb, with a view opening out to more woodland up ahead. The pleasant green lane arrives at a road and the route continues straight on towards

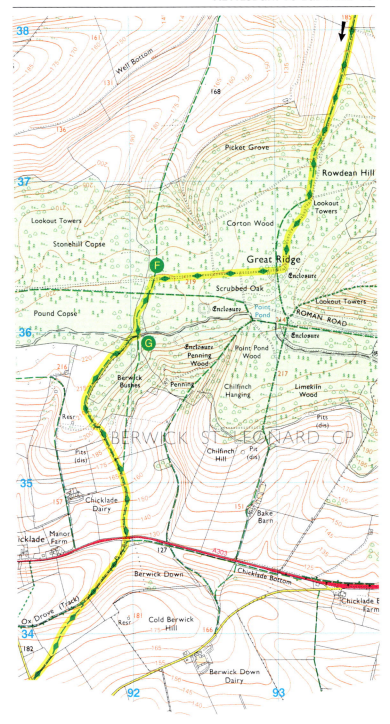

the village of Hindon, dominated by its tall church spire **17**. Just before reaching the village **H** turn right onto the narrow footpath running between fences, then continue across the field, cross two stiles and turn left down the wide village street. This is an appealing place with an interesting mixture of houses, predominantly brick or tile hung, with a penchant for dormer windows. Not surprisingly, given its position at a major cross roads, it has its share of inns, one of which The Grosvenor Arms still advertises good stabling and lock-up coach houses. Carry straight on at the cross roads to the junction at the end of the village street, turn right and then immediately take the left hand fork. Where the houses end **I** turn right onto the track. Where paths cross **J** turn left onto the very wide track heading towards the woods.

The track narrows down as it climbs up into the trees. The path keeps near the edge of this fine wood, with its tall beech interspersed with coppice. Reaching an old pit, the path finally levels out briefly, before plunging downhill. Emerging from the trees, continue straight on down

A track winds its way through the trees on Rowdean Hill, but the route is not always this clear in the woods.

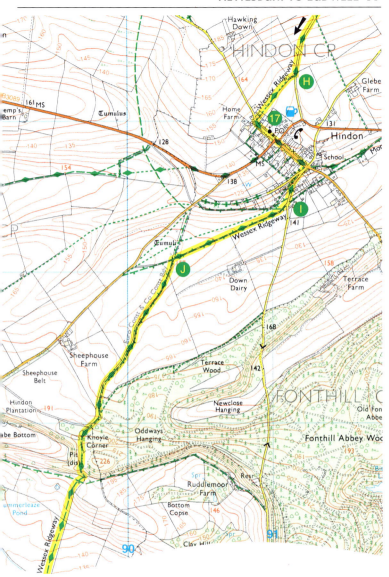

the green track, with a view of a higgledy-piggledy pattern of trees and the prospect of still more hills rising up ahead, as the village of East Knoyle comes into view on the right. This grassy path is a particular delight for those who come this way in a wet season, which can turn the woodland paths into a quagmire. Nearing the foot of the hill, the track runs briefly to the right by a hedge, left through a field gate – and

then left again through a gate in the hedge **K**. The way now runs beside the hedge across the fields to join a little stream that runs in from the left. From here turn right to a gate by the road.

At the road turn left past Cools Cottage, then just before the road turns left, turn right through a metal gate and go straight across the field towards the nearest point on the wood that stretches down the hill, passing to the left of a small copse of trees. Coming up the hill, a metal gate comes into view by a new plantation. Follow the track up through the trees to reach a wooden gate to the left of the path, beyond which a field path leads up beside the woods, and the summit of the hill is finally reached at the road, after a stiff little climb of almost 100 metres. There is therefore every excuse to pause to look back and enjoy the view before crossing the road to admire the equally enticing vista in the opposite direction. Go through the farm gate and take the track to the left, heading towards the houses. At the road **L** turn right, then right again, passing a converted church, now a private house and look out for a signpost on the left to find a stile quite hidden away inside the hedge and cross the field to a stile opposite. At the edge of the woods, heavy with the smell of garlic from dense clumps of ramson, take the path that wanders rather aimlessly off to the right through the trees and then meanders through the woodland fringe. The route drops down through wooden steps to a stile, and the woodland ends with a view down to a lovely sheltered farmhouse, snugly wrapped in wooded hills. Continue through two gates and turn left onto the path by the side of the wood, with a splendid vista of hills, each with its own individual crown of trees.

Cross a stile **M** and take the path following the line of the fence, then left down the field as indicated by a marker arrow. Take the wide track to the left of the barn, still continuing downhill. Cross straight over the road and take the path across the field by the fence to rejoin the road further on **N**. Turn left to cross the railway – the Salisbury to Exeter line this time – and then turn left by a footpath sign to cross a field and a footbridge to the road. Turn left at the road by the primary school, then right at the first junction signposted to Wardour Castle **18** and continue straight on into the grounds. Follow the drive round in front of the house, built in a frigid, classical style, somewhat alleviated by an airy chapel at one end. Turn left towards an iron gate, cross a stile and take the green track heading towards Old Wardour Castle **19**.

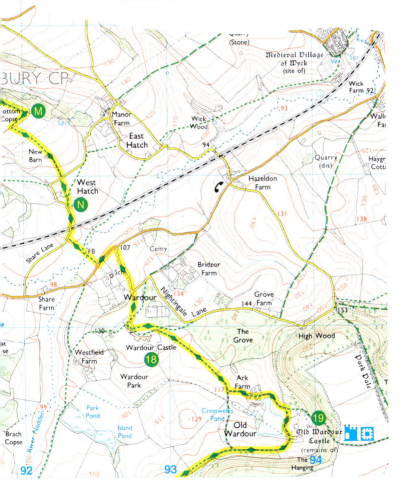

The romantic ruins of Old Wardour Castle stand right beside the walk, and the temptation to stop off for a closer look is irresistible.

Where the track divides, take the path to the left through the farm-yard to the old castle, which is open to the public. It is an extraordinary place, as dramatic as the new castle is dull. The centrepiece is the hexagonal building of the 14th century, full of odd classical detailing. Later owners felt it was not sufficiently romantic in itself and added a Gothic pavilion and grotto to the grounds.

The track continues round the large lake, and where the track divides by a gateway, keep to the right. Looking back at the new castle, it turns out to be rather better than it seemed at close quarters, for all the decorative effects have been kept to the south facade, with a bold central pediment and pilasters. The way continues by the side of a wood, and looking back at the castle rising above the lake presents a scene that would have gladdened the heart of any 18th century seeker-out of the picturesque. Leaving the woods behind, the track continues beside parkland to arrive at another tree-fringed lake, one in a chain of five. Beyond this, cross a stile and head slightly right towards a gate in front of the wood. The path now turns right, a broad forest ride, through close-packed conifers. Where the path immediately divides **O** keep to the right past a watchtower.

Leaving the wood, continue on the gravel drive between houses down to the road and turn left. At the road junction **P** turn right to head downhill on another typical deep-sunk lane. Cross the stream and turn

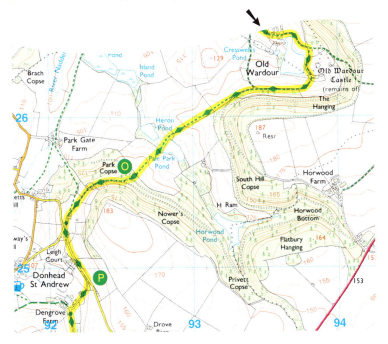

left onto a concrete track that, at first, winds gently uphill. Soon, however, it steepens, the concrete ends and the way continues as a deep-cut path sheltered by a tall hedge. Reaching the road **Q** turn right and immediately left onto a footpath going downhill beside the houses, and straight along the road opposite marked as a dead end. Go through a metal gate and take the path in the field beside the fence on the right, with Ludwell church providing a prominent landmark to the right. A newly layered hedge provides an attractive accompaniment as the track swings past a beautiful stone farmhouse with mullioned windows. Turn left and right to cross the stream that runs in from the left. Turn right on the road and immediately left to take the byway past the prominent radio mast. Just before the houses, turn left onto the footpath to the main road at Ludwell.

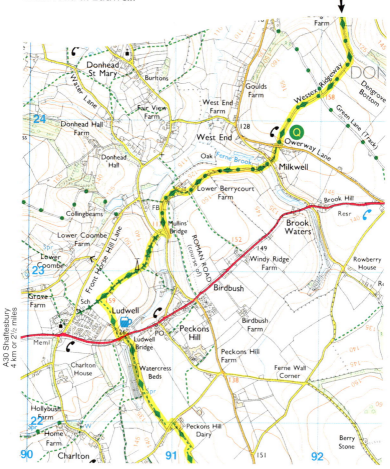

The farming landscape near Donhead St Andrew still retains its old patterns of fields and hedgerows.

CIRCULAR WALK TO UPTON LOVELL

5 miles (8 km)

The walk begins by turning left off the Way at Knook (p.72) to cross the footbridge **A**. Continue on up to the village and turn right by the ancient church of St Margaret, mainly Norman, but with Anglo-Saxon carving inside and a curious blocked doorway on the southern wall with more carvings, this time with a very Celtic flavour. Continue on, past an imposing square house with an unusually large hipped roof in thatch, towards the village of Upton Lovell.

Continue through the village and follow the road round to the left **B**: the church with its short square tower can be seen over to the right. At the junction cross straight over the main road passing the house known as The Folly which still has a small well in front. Follow the byway, which climbs steeply up to the farm buildings. Here the surfaced road gives way to a rough track, with extensive views over the typical soft, swooping curves of downland, alternating with pallid, chalky hollows. Cross the road and continue straight on towards the flat, open land of Salisbury Plain. To the right of the track are the earthworks of Knook Castle, clearly not a defensive system, but one containing a settlement. Around it, close to the track, are more earthworks suggestive of tracks and enclosures.

The track ends at the Army firing range **C**. Turn left along the track, passing a number of tumuli, including a substantial long barrow, on the right. Where the track begins to dip downhill, turn left **D** onto a grassy track, signposted as a byway. This offers splendid walking on soft turf with immense views. Turn right at the fence in front of the old barn **E** and head off past the reservoir. Where the army camp comes into view follow the track which sweeps round the edge of the deep combe and then swings right towards the barn **F**. Turn left onto the downhill track beside the wood and continue past the camp to the road. Turn right at the road and follow it round, along the A36. Where the pavement ends **G** cross over to the footpath opposite and turn immediately left up the stone steps. Go through the kissing gate to take the path by the side of the woods down to the river. Continue on the attractive riverside walk, past a broken weir and a tin shack containing a three-cylinder water-powered engine once used for pumping water to the village and for generating electricity.

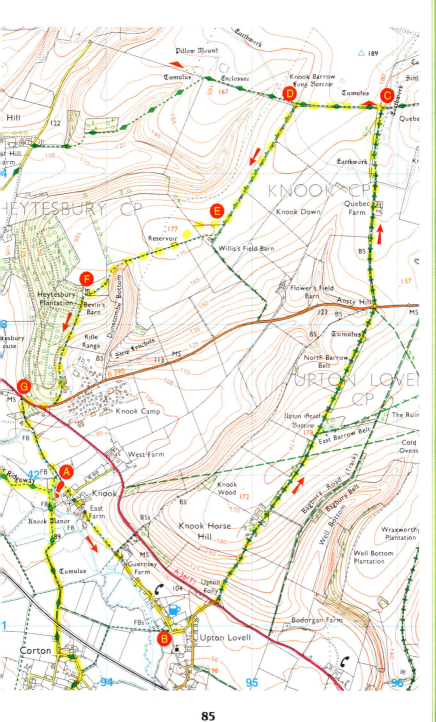

85

Sinuous curves mark the landscape, where the cultivated land of the valley reaches t

3h grass of the downland at Win Green.

5 LUDWELL TO SHILLINGSTONE

via Tollard Royal and Iwerne Courtney 14 ½ miles (23.5 km)

Turn left along the road towards the Grove Arms, and take the track opposite, passing extensive watercress beds **20**, which are arranged at different levels to allow a steady but gentle flow of water through the system. By a shed on the right, cross a stile to take the grassy footpath, still following the line of the beds. Where a fence appears on the right, turn left over a stile on a narrow path beside a tall hedge. At the road **A** turn left and immediately right on the track past the farm buildings, heading straight up the field towards a little gate. Continue up the grassland with a hedge to the left. The path now goes straight through the middle of a field of crops, as shown by the direction arrow at the stile. This is fine open countryside of gentle undulations, with a more definite line of hills striding across the horizon.

An Edwardian railway carriage finds a new use as a hen house.

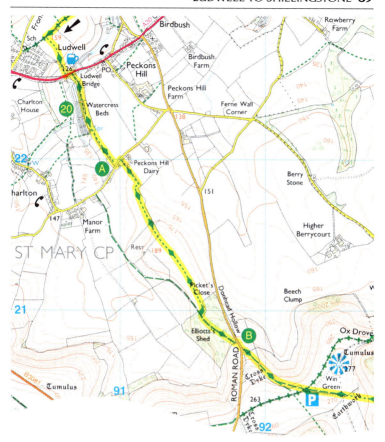

The path enters a wood and joins with a broader track heading straight through. At the road **B** turn right, then immediately left by the bridleway sign. Cross a stile and head off on a diagonal to the right across the face of the hill. There are no obvious landmarks at first, until you see a fence curving round the end of a deep hollow. Follow this round to a stile that leads to a broad track and turn left towards the car park. As always, the effort of reaching the top of the escarpment is rewarded by superb views, and these are as good as any met along the way – a billowing of hills, rising and falling and spreading out into the far distance. Go through the car park and take the grassy track with the fence to your right. Now the fine views are matched by the delight of walking over soft turf. The view opens to the right over a wide plain, while up ahead there is attractive woodland – it is the sort of country-side any walker would be happy to roll up and take away for future use.

Tollard Royal Church and the thirteenth-century hunting lodge, King John's House, seen from the circular walk.

Cross a stile on the right and follow the fence until the ground falls away steeply towards a wood. Take an indistinct path down the ridge to the right and then follow a wire fence downhill to find a gate into the wood. From here, a much more obvious track can be followed down through the trees. Reaching the valley floor after the steep descent, turn right onto a broad, stony track **C**. There could hardly be a greater contrast than that between the uplands recently left behind and this secluded, wooded hollow where nothing disturbs the peace but the harsh, strident calls of pheasants. The woodland climbs the bank to either side, and a small farm seems almost lost among the trees. The walk continues down the farm approach road. Where the track divides **D** carry straight on through the gate. The valley gradually opens out, with soft green slopes to either side. Where tracks divide by a metal fence **E** turn left to head down the deeply scooped out green valley. At the end of another very pleasant section, go round the farmyard on the left to a track which turns right to Tollard Royal. It emerges by a pond **21**, well stocked with fish and overlooked by a charming thatched cottage. This is the start of a circular walk through Chase Woods (see p.98).

Turn right along the road towards the village, then right again past the Post Office onto a broad, stony track. At the houses, carry straight on along the green track, with the fence to the right. There is a long steady climb, overlooking the valley you have just walked down, and seen from a different viewpoint the effect is quite different but just as beautiful. Turn right at the road **F** which continues to offer superb and dramatic views over to the right as the land tumbles away into deep hollows. Where the road levels out **G**, look for a stile in the hedge on the left.Cross over and head diagonally across the field to a signpost

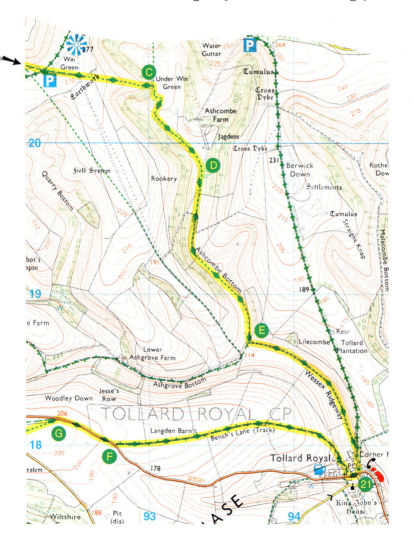

on the far side. Cross the road to a stile opposite, heading towards the village and find the stile in the hedge. After crossing two stiles take the obvious broad track that runs into Ashmore by an encouraging sign announcing that walkers on the Wessex Ridgeway now only have 62 miles to go to reach Lyme Regis. It also marks a boundary, where the Way leaves Wiltshire and enters Dorset.

At the village **H** turn right and go round the village pond to take the road round to the left. Go past the church and take the bridleway on the left, leading out over the wide open spaces of Cranborne Chase. Partridges are quite common, scuttling away at a surprisingly fast if slightly comical run. The path heads off through a patch of woodland, with a wider expanse of trees ranged behind it. On reaching the larger wood of typically densely planted conifers, continue straight on passing one track junction to the edge of the trees, then turn right **I** keeping to the woodland fringe. The route now goes steadily downhill. At the foot of the slope, turn right into a coppice, then turn almost immediately left **J** by a waymarked footpath sign to head back uphill again. Wood anemones brighten the way as a stiff climb leads to the edge of the wood. Continue on the field path beside the trees, and take the broad path that swings downhill again to the road **K**.

Looking back to Iwerne Courtney from Hambledon Hill.

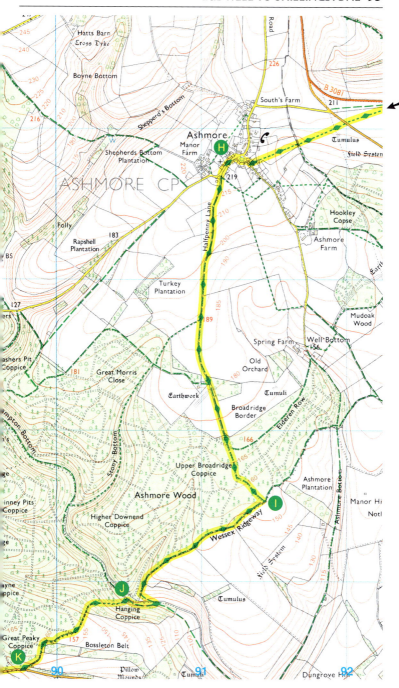

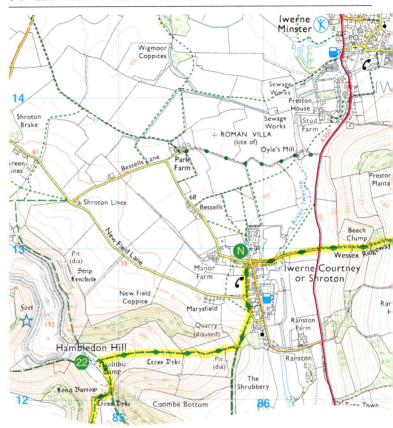

Turn right along the road and at the far side of the woods on the left **L** turn left onto the bridleway. Where the tracks divide, follow the main route round to the left. This is a very attractive section, with widely spaced, broad-leaved trees, leaving ample room for woodland flowers. Emerging from the trees, turn right onto the path at the edge of the field. This is a notably flinty area, with large nodules poking up above the ground. Cross the road, turn left and immediately right onto the next woodland track. There is a brief opening out to a wide view before one is plunged into a close-packed plantation. On leaving the woods there is a prospect of more hills up ahead and a view to the left of the ramparted summit of Hod Hill, one of the few forts in the region that this walk does not visit. Stay with this track, passing a hollow on the left, with more patches of woodland providing the dominant note in the scene. Where the farm track swings left at the end of the first field **M** carry straight on along the grassy track beside the hedge. Coming to the top

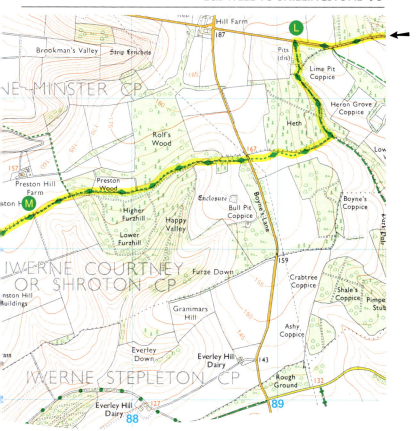

of the ridge the village with two names – both Iwerne Courtney or Shroton being, it seems, equally acceptable – comes into view. The path heads steeply downhill towards it, a comfortable looking spot with its prominent church sitting under the sheltering bulk of Hambledon Hill.

At the major road, continue straight on along the minor road into the village. At the crossroads **N** take the footpath by the old bakery which winds round the backs of the houses. Turn left at the road, then right onto the bridleway, immediately beyond the cricket pavilion with its appropriate cricketing weather vane. Join the chalk track that leads uphill passing through the metal gate. Follow the line of the wall, and where that ends, turn right onto the obvious track heading straight up the hill. After a long, unremitting climb the ramparts of the huge fort of Hambledon Hill come into view, some of the most impressive of any met along the way. Reaching the top of the hill by a trig point **22** there is a complete panorama with an immense overview of a richly varied

A great sweep of downland seen from the ramparts and ditches that circle Hambledon Hill.

countryside: vales and woodland, escarpment edge and isolated hills. This was also the site of one of the more bizarre incidents of the Civil War. A group of local countrymen, disenchanted with the ravages of the armies, declared that they would let neither side near. Armed only with clubs – earning themselves the name of Clubmen – they defied Cromwell's troops and were predictably routed in August 1645.

Turn left onto the broad, grassy track, with a view down to a large quarry that has slashed a white scar across the face of the hill. Nearer at hand on the right is a system of banks marking the edge of a causewayed camp, dated to between 2900 and 2600 BC, which seems to have been a great Neolithic graveyard. The track goes down to a wooden gate and turns right beside the fence. The path soon begins to go very steeply downhill. At the bottom of the field, turn left beside the wire fence and from here there is a good view back to the hill fort. Go through a metal gate, and turn right to reach the road by a neat little lodge **O**. Turn left at the road and then right at the next junction, down the road marked as 'No Through Road'. The route passes a fine, old, gabled house, with an impressive array of tall chimneys, now a school. Where the way divides near the house **P** turn right on the bridleway that turns off just before the farm. Go through the farmyard and continue in the same direction to go through another gate and take the grassy path down to the river.

Turn left onto the path down through the coppice with the occasional gleam of water from the busy River Stour. On leaving the wood, turn right through a gate to reach the footbridge **Q**, where the river is revealed as free-flowing but muddied to the colour of milky coffee. Cross the bridge and head left towards the gate at the end of the line of trees. Go down the farm track and carry straight on along the road under the old railway bridge **23**. This once carried the old Somerset and Dorset Joint Railway and is a fine example of the bricklayer's art. Because the bridge was built on a skew, the bricks are laid in long, sloping diagonals. At the road turn right towards the houses at the edge of Shillingstone.

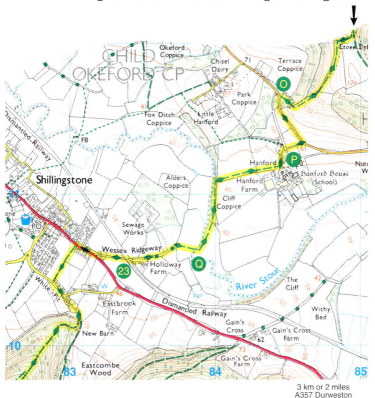

3 km or 2 miles
A357 Durweston

CIRCULAR WALK IN CHASE WOODS

6 miles (10 km)

The walk starts at the pond in Tollard Royal **21**. Turn left, away from the village, down the road past a small well on the right with the inscription 'With Thee is the well of life'. Just past the road sign **A** turn left up a slope to a gate with a yellow arrow and take the track that leads uphill at an angle from the road. At the top of the hill, which gives a good view back to King John's House, turn left past a tall stand of beech, heading for the trees that provide shelter for a farmhouse. Cross over the ridge and carry on downhill to the woodland. At the fence **B** turn right to follow the path beside the wood. This is very pleasant walking along a path lined with massive oaks.

Go through the gate to the road **C** and immediately turn left on the route marked 'Private Road – Footpath Only'. Where the way divides, turn slightly to the right of the obvious track to cross the parkland by a series of stiles. Cross straight over the driveway and take the obvious green track into the woods. Where the path immediately divides, go to the right as shown by a yellow arrow. The woods are a mixture of conifers, mature beech and coppice. The air is loud with birdsong and there are frequent glimpses of deer among the trees. The path swings round to the right passing a high brick wall, with tantalizing glimpses of turrets and cupolas behind it. It emerges onto a golf course, and continues at the edge of the wood with immense views to the south.

At the end of the wall **D** continue following the edge of the golf course, passing in front of the ornamental gates and continue down into a hollow where a small lake provides a daunting golf hazard. Beyond the thatched cottage, take the path between the fence and the wood, which eventually swings away to head through the trees, passing three fine old oaks, with conifers to the left and coppice to the right. The path dips down to a long straight ride in a hollow and continues straight on. Where the way divides by a new conifer plantation, carry straight on. At the next major track crossing **E** turn left by a post with a blue arrow. The path goes close to the centre circle where the formal, tree-lined rides meet. Continue on passing the end of another parade of trees, known as The General's Avenue. The track swings round a clearing to reach the end of the wood and then curves away to join the road **F**.

Turn left at the road. Just before the ornamental gates with two fine Jacobean-style lodges **G** turn right to cross the stile, continue through a gate and turn left to follow the track at the edge of the wood. The coppice to the left is almost crowded with strolling pheasants. The route heads steadily downhill along the rim of a deep valley, then there is a steep dip to the valley floor. Beyond a tall metal gate, go straight forward to the next gate **H**. Turn half right to follow the line of the fence uphill. Just beyond the edge of the trees, turn right to cross a stile and take the path at the side of the field. Beyond the end of a long stand of beech, take the path that dips down through the trees to return to the start.

Scale is approx 2¼ inches to 1 mile

99

6 SHILLINGSTONE TO SYDLING ST NICHOLAS

via Giant's Head   *18¹⁄₂ miles (30 km)*

Immediately beyond the first row of houses on the left, turn left **A** down the path heading towards the now prominent quarry. Turn left onto the road and right at the road junction. At the top of a steep little hill **B** turn right off the road for a very steep path heading through the wood. Constant use has cut this path deep down to the chalky bedrock, creating a narrow way for one of the longest and steepest climbs of the whole route, rising eventually to a summit at 223 metres (731 ft). The deer that populate this wood make far lighter work of bounding around the hills than the slow, plodding walker.

The intimate landscape of hedge fields and woods below Bulbarrow Hill.

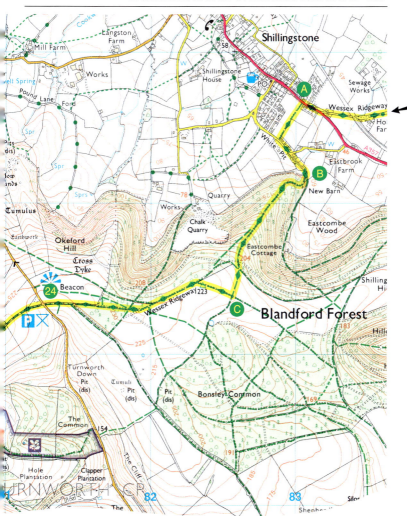

Cross a broad forest track and leave the woods, heading straight out across the field to a marker post **C**. Turn right past the trig point, signalling that the climb has finally ended, and rejoin the broad, green track at the edge of the wood. Where the track divides by a large patch of gorse, take the path that leads back through the trees, but soon re-emerges to run along the opposite side of the wood. Up ahead is a beacon, in the form of a large fire basket on top of a tall pole **24**. Cross over the road to the car park and picnic area and continue along the obvious track beside a hedge.

The view soon opens out over the plain and back over Hambledon Hill, while there is a fine prospect up ahead as the Way follows the meandering escarpment edge. There is the familiar contrast between the rough ground of the hills and the neat patterns of fields and blocks of woodland down below. The track goes downhill to meet a road **D**. Turn left and promptly begin the climb back up again. The road passes a house called Bakers Folly, which was once a restaurant, and boasted in its advert that it offered not just good food but the best view in Dorset. The food is now past comment, but anyone coming this way can certainly vouch for the view. Those who want to know just what they are seeing can have their curiosity satisfied at the viewpoint **25** where the inscribed table points to places as far away as Glastonbury Tor and the Quantocks. There is also an inscription from one of Thomas Hardy's poems and a quotation from *Tess of the d'Urbervilles*.

At the road junction turn right and keep to the right as the road divides. There is a tempting grassy area here that seems to demand that you sit down and wallow in the vista across Blackmoor Vale. After this the view is temporarily lost behind trees. Continue straight on at the next junction and, as yet another hill fort comes into sight, there is an attractive prospect over to the left of lakes in a little valley. The road goes downhill, and just before reaching the fort **E**, turn left through a metal gate to take the hollow way that goes round the outside of the fort, Rawlsbury Camp **26**. It enjoys a dramatic situation, with a tall, sculpted cross rising above the ramparts.

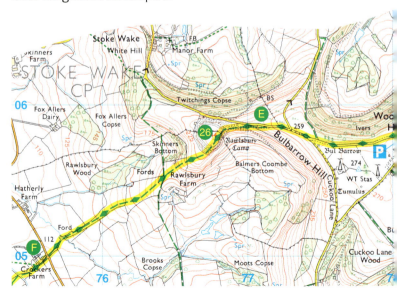

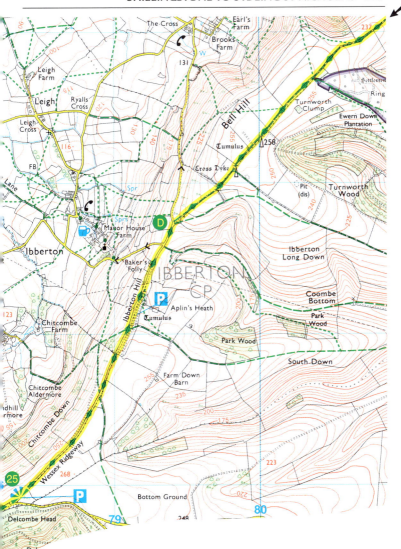

As the ramparts begin to turn, head downhill through a metal gate at the end of a long line of beech and continue down the field towards the distant farm. Go through a couple of gates, but near the bottom of the hill, after passing through a metal gate, do not head straight on towards the next gate but head slightly to the left where the field funnels down towards a small stream. Ford the stream, continue on the track down to the road and cross straight over onto the bridleway beside the farm **F**. Where the concrete farm track swings right, go

The hamlet of Minterne Parva: the building on the right is thought to have held a cock pit.

straight on through the gate and head off towards the top left hand side of the next field, take another diagonal route across the next field, then carry straight on to a track junction **G** and turn left towards the woodland. Take the path just inside the wood, beyond which it gives way to a farm approach road.

Follow the bridleway through the farmyard, go uphill past the barns to a metal gate **H** and turn right onto the path by the hedge. The path leads up a steep, wooded ridge, keeping to the crest and heading towards a prominent stand of conifers. Once clear of the trees, Blackmoor Vale, comes into sight again, while to the left there is a gentle roll of hills. The path dips down to the left of the ridge to a meeting of tracks in what is known as the Dorsetshire Gap. Those who walk this route are invited to sign their names in a book kept in a tin box by the gate. Go through the gate and take the track going slightly uphill past the prominent mound and signposted to Folly. A hollow way climbs back up to another ridge and then veers off to the left through the trees. Leave the woods by the metal gate and continue straight forward, a water tank silhouetted on the horizon providing a convenient way marker.

The Way has arrived at another hilltop, with yet more earthworks over to the right. This is a promontory fort **27**. The steep slopes round three sides constitute the main defence with rampart and ditch built across the neck of land to complete the ring. At the far side of the field **I** turn right to join a little lane between rough hedges, that begins to go downhill, but already the next hill can be seen, ensuring that the next climb is not far away. Continue downhill, with smoothly moulded grassland to the right falling away to chalky edges.

The road is joined at Folly, where disappointingly there is no folly of any sort on view. Cross straight over and inevitably there is a long, uphill slog, this time to a small wood. Happily, with equal inevitability, the reward for the effort comes in the shape of more superb scenery. Close at hand is a gorse-spattered hillside, below which are the banks of an old field system, while the long view is of a steady repetition of wooded hills, standing guard over farms snuggled down in the hollows. The walking is now particularly pleasant on soft turf with a hedge to the right. The path passes above a wood, clambering up the hillside and continues straight on across the next field. It swings to the left passing an early enclosure, difficult to date in an area where medieval and Iron Age earthworks intermingle, defined by prominent banks **28**. The route continues on the open top of the ridge, looking down on the farmland and the cosily situated village that seems to live up to its name, Plush.

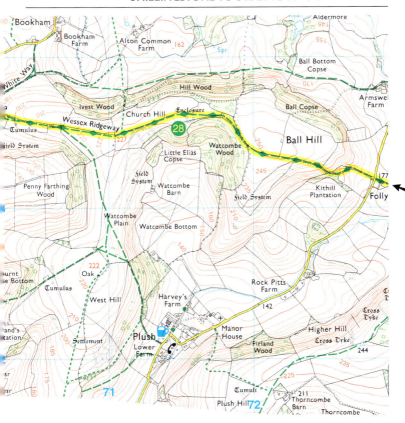

The way continues along a farm track between fields and hedges, still enjoying a very open aspect. Soon the next descent begins, diagonally downhill to the left, on a heading towards the left of the white house in the valley. Follow the hollow way beside the hedge to the road **J**, turn left and immediately right onto the farm road and continue on the bridleway heading uphill between hedges. The summit provides the expected viewpoint, but one of the delights of this part of the walk is the way in which there are subtle changes from one summit to the next. The Vale has been left behind, and now there is just the steady, rhythmic rise and fall of hills that makes this an area of such richly varied beauty. Where tracks divide at a low barn **K**, carry straight on through a metal gate. Go through a second gate at the top of the field and turn right towards the campsite. Follow the perimeter path round to the road **L**. Cross straight on to continue along the way, but those wanting to take the walk down through Cerne Abbas turn left (see p.112).

After leaving the road, look for a gate in the hedge **M** and turn right. The path heads across the fields towards a prominent, single tree, beyond which a gate leads to a path going downhill. Coming out through the line of scrub there is a view of fields formed into sinuous boundaries by the wavelike front of the escarpment. The way down is past a marker post, heading towards the little settlement of Minterne Parva. The path runs just above the hedge on the left for a little way, then turns left through a gate. It now heads straight downhill to a solitary tree, beyond which a farm track leads to the hamlet **30**. For such a tiny place, it has a great deal of interest. The track passes a square house, with an unusually tall, two-storey semicircular bay. At the crossroads turn left on the road marked as 'No Through Road' past an odd circular building with a conical roof, which according to local tradition once housed cock fights.

The road becomes a sunken lane between tree-topped banks. Cross a busy, little stream and go through woodland to the junction **N**. Turn right and left at the junction towards Up Cerne. The road goes downhill past an array of beautiful beech trees. On the left is the manor house, church and parkland where swans on the lake complete the perfect, picturesque scene which the landscaper no doubt had in mind. The minor

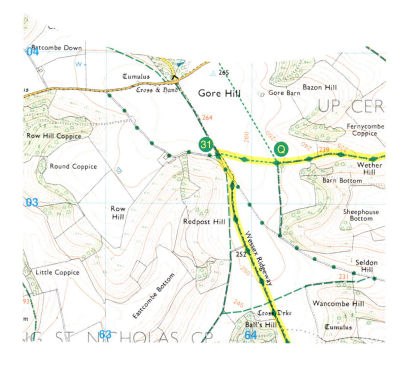

road itself is a delight with flowers massing along the bank. Just beyond the typically uniform estate cottages, cross the stream and turn right by the shelter **O**. The road runs up between fields with a stream for accompaniment, up a lovely valley which seems to have contrived to hide itself away from the rest of the world. The road gives way to a rough track passing a small copse, beyond which **P** the way turns left for one more climb through the fields. Nearing the top of the hill, the song of the skylark which had been an almost constant companion over the Wiltshire Downs, returns once again. There is still an air of great secrecy about this landscape, where little lonely valleys creep out from the hills.

Reaching the top, the track leads on between two patches of woodland. Where the bridleway swings left by a circle of trees **Q** continue along the footpath across the field. Go through the hedge and suddenly and dramatically the land simply drops away in front of you, falling off into a beautiful, narrow, deep valley. Here, as if acknowledging that this really is one of the very special places along the way is a tall, splendidly isolated signpost **31**. The track now swings round to the left above the edge, and where the track divides continue straight on. There are no

1 km or ¹/₂ mile
A352 Cerne Abbas

route finding problems to worry about for some way as the track keeps to the ridge and heads straight off towards a distant radio mast. A slight kink in the track provides a small variation, but no one could be bored with this section with its airy openness and exhilarating outlook. Eventually, after passing the mast, the path dips down to reach the road but still continues straight forward on the farm track.

The long straight ends at the farm **R**. Turn right between the barns. At the top of the hill, an immense pile of flints gives a good indication of just how stony this land is and why for centuries it was considered far more suitable as pasture than arable. Follow the track as it swings round to the right and now Sydling St Nicholas **32** comes into sight. Turn right for the path beside the hedge which soon begins to go steeply downhill to join a farm track. This eventually reaches a lane running between hedges that leads down to the village.

The old petrol pump is just one of the many features that make Sydling St Nicholas a village of immense charm.

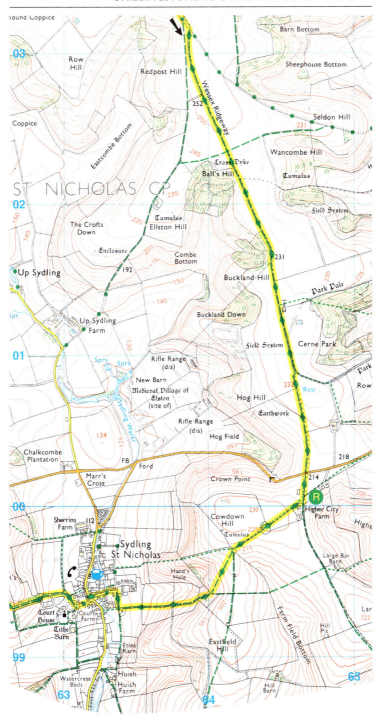

Circular walk to Cerne Abbas

2¹/₂ miles (4 km)

Turn left along the road from the camp site. Just beyond the milestone, turn right through the farm gate by a sign with a blue arrow **A**. Take the field path by the hedge on the right. At the end of the field turn left to the escarpment edge marked by gorse bushes. An obvious track cut deep into the chalk runs diagonally down the slope of the ridge. At the path division **B** take the path to the right and turn right along the path beside the road into Cerne Abbas. The village is an obvious tourist attraction, but it wears its charm with ease, a happy jumble of styles and periods, with stone and flint next to timber framing and a spattering of Georgian formality. The church, with its splendid Perpendicular tower, dominates, but sadly little is left of the Abbey originally founded in the 9th century apart from the former gatehouse, now Abbey House.

At the road junction **C** turn right on the riverside path, where bright patches of marsh marigolds look down over lazily waving weeds in the stream. Turn right over the bridge, then left onto the farm track to come

The famous Cerne Abbas giant.

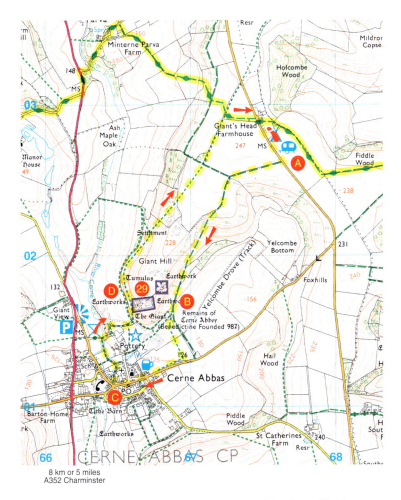

8 km or 5 miles
A352 Charminster

out immediately beneath the famous hill figure of The Giant **29**. No accurate date has ever been fixed, but he is generally agreed to be Roman, probably depicting Hercules and certainly a fertility symbol. The track now wriggles round the farm, and on reaching an open field turn right to follow it round beneath The Giant. Go through a wooden gate on the right **D** to join a narrow path through the scrub, and turn left to follow a track heading up across the shoulder of the hill to another patch of scrub. The path continues as a prickly passage through thorn and holly, then heads uphill to pass above gorse bushes. Cross a stile and take the track towards the barn and continue along the edge of the field. Where tall trees appear in the hedge on the left there is a gate leading back to the Wessex Ridgeway coming down from the main road.

113

7 SYDLING ST NICHOLAS TO BEAMINSTER

via Maiden Newton   *14 miles (22.5 km)*

Reaching the houses at the edge of the village, turn right to arrive at a little green and carry on down the road, turning left to reach the High Street. It is a village well worth exploring, so picturesque it could have been designed by the tourist board, but really proving no more than the lasting appeal of vernacular architecture at is best. Turn right by the old cross **A** and continue on towards the church, but before reaching it follow the road round to the right by the brick wall for the track somewhat ominously signposted as Break Heart Hill. The path swings left and begins a steep climb, along which the walker is

The view from Break Heart Hill: the Way goes straight through the middle of this attractive landscape.

encouraged – or is it mocked? – by the inhabitants of the local rookery. There is a short respite as the path dips down, only to be followed by an even steeper climb up to the traffic on the main road. A narrow track runs between hedgerows and this comes out onto a grassy slope which is climbed with the hedge and fence on the left. Go through an iron gate and continue on to the road. This is the A37, which follows the line of the old Roman road over Break Heart Hill.

Cross straight over the road to the bridleway opposite, a splendid upland route where buzzards soar and mew overhead. The track is now a long, straight line, running past a barn, once converted into a house, but

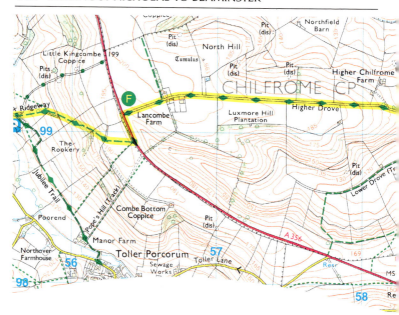

now considerably the worse for wear. Go through a metal gate and the grassland returns and a grand scene opens up in front. Up ahead is Maiden Newton, while over to the right is an array of masts that will become a familiar feature over the next few miles. Beyond a wooden gate **B** turn right onto the track that leads downhill. Go under the railway bridge by the neat, pleasantly unpretentious station **33** on the line down to Weymouth. At the road junction, turn left, then right by the war memorial to pass the church. It retains many medieval features, and ferocious gargoyles frown down below the crenellated parapet, as though defying visitors. Head towards the farmyard, turn left over a stile to take the path round the churchyard, then immediately right by the barn **C** on the path signposted to Chilfrome.

The path dips down into scrubby woodland beside the infant River Frome. Cross a footbridge and turn right on the riverside path, where sluice gates can be seen controlling the water flow. Turn left along the embankment and go under the arch of the disused Bridport branch line.

Continue on the path by the river, now overhung by willow. Cross a tributary stream, then turn left **D** beside a marshy area of pallid reeds. Follow the line of the hedge on the right to cross a stile and turn right to follow the path round the field to another stile on the right. Cross a little footbridge over a ditch and head straight across the field to a metal gate and a Wessex Ridgeway signpost which has a map reference to confirm exactly where you are. The path, in fact, emerges by the appealing, if plain, little church of Chilfrome **34**. It is surprising that it

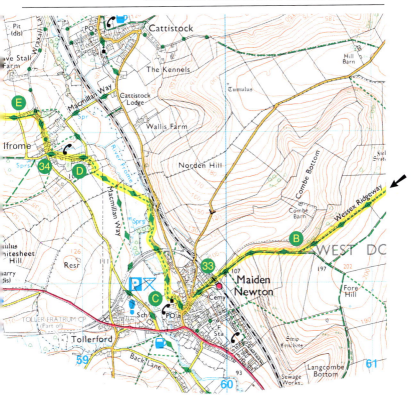

exists at all, for just down the road is the altogether grander Cattistock church, with an immense tower, not medieval but Victorian, the work of George Gilbert Scott, son of the famous Gothic revivalist.

Continue past the church and turn right at the crossroads by the telephone box. Following a steep climb, turn sharp left onto a bridle-way which soon swings to the right. At the road **E** turn right. This is a typical country lane running between hedges, and one of the few long stretches of road walking along the whole way. It carries on dead straight, gently climbing and rather featureless, finally levelling out where a long line of trees comes in from the right. Now the radio installation seen earlier looms large on the horizon, and as the hedges give way to fences so the view begins to open out. Turn left at the main road **F** and where it begins to swing left, go through a gate on the right by a bridleway sign. Do not take the obvious track, but turn half right to cross the field to a gate, beyond which the path leads straight over the next field. This leads on to a narrow path through the patch of scrub climbing up the slope. Carry on along the same line

Old mill sluice gear at Maiden Newton, cast at nearby Beaminster in 1857.

through two more fields. The path runs beside a line of trees and a ditch and where that ends turn half left to pass a solitary tree and head for the barn. Go through the gate in the hedge, turn left and then right onto the track down to the road at Lower Kingcombe. This is an interesting area, for the land here was owned by the same family for three generations and remained virtually unchanged. In 1987 much of the land was taken over by the Dorset Wildlife Trust, and the Kingcombe Trust established an information centre and residential visitor centre in the old farm buildings. It provides a rare opportunity to see what meadows were once like, with an abundance of wild flowers, including orchids, which in turn attract many species of rare butterflies.

The information centre is to the left **35** but the road turns right past the thatched cottages. Where the road turns left, carry straight on up the bridleway which soon becomes a rough, stony track sunk between high banks rich in flowers. Leaving the path by the old gate, turn half left to the gate giving access to the wood **36**. This is a managed wood with a good deal of new planting and, what is now a rarity, a worked coppice, where the hazel is regularly harvested for hurdle making. A green track runs through the edge of the coppice, and then continues straight ahead across the bottom of the slope on the right, heading straight for the radio masts which have been a landmark for so long. Rounding the hill on the right, head towards the gate that stands just below the masts **G** and turn right onto the road. Turn left in front of the transmission station boundary onto the green way, an area extremely popular with rabbits that scamper backwards and forwards between the banks. The top of the hill overlooks rolling farmland, with farms dotted around, each to its own protective hollow. Having reached this point, the track promptly heads back down the other side following the hedge on the right. Turn half left at the next field to pass the corner that sticks out into the middle, heading for a farm track by a solitary tree. Go through a metal gate and follow the line of the hedge on the left to the road, with the village of Hooke over to the left.

Cross straight over the road onto the green track opposite, which arrives at a system of ponds, and as this is Mill Lane, one can reasonably assume that they did indeed once serve a mill. Cross over the stream, turn left at the road **H** and then right at the junction by

another large pond with a number of ducks and coots making their homes in the reeds. Pass St Francis Farm which, as befits its name, has a particularly large bird table. Across the road is grand Hooke Court, mainly 17th century and now an educational establishment. The recent additions, however, have all the charm of an army barracks. There are yet more ponds, with more exotic inhabitants, including a black swan. Just beyond this, go through a gate on the right **I** and turn diagonally left up the slope of the field towards the corner of the wood. Cross a stile and follow the edge of what the map names as a coppice, but which is now hopelessly overgrown and tangled, although popular with the tuneful birds hidden in its depths. At the corner of the field turn right to cross a stile rather hidden among the trees and head for the left hand corner turning right onto the road.

Canada geese enjoying life on one of the tree-shaded ponds at Toller Whelme.

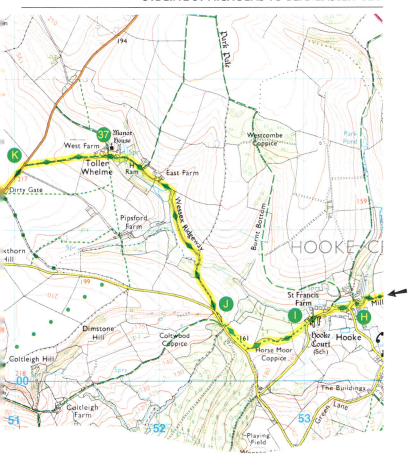

At the top of a steep little hill take the 'No Through Road' sign-posted to Toller Whelme **J**. This typical West Country lane dives down to a small stream and promptly climbs back up again. There is a reedy lake down to the left, then a much larger pond with a range of wild-fowl including Canada geese and pochard. On reaching the houses the road gives way to a rough track, passing yet another pond with ducks and the splendid thatched manor house **37** with, unusually for this area, stone slate in part of the roof. With its mullioned windows and Gothic arches it is everything a romantic manor should be. Here the track turns off to the left. Go through a metal gate to join a green track that narrows down to a footpath running beside a tall hedge. At the road **K** turn left, and at the first junction right onto the 'No Through Road' to Langdon.

This runs along the top of the hill with a view of the next main objective, Beaminster down on the left. Where the surfaced road turns right **L** carry straight on along the rough track, still keeping to the escarpment edge, and cross straight over the road onto the path beside the hedge. At the next road **M** turn left, then left again by a signpost saying 'Buckham Down', passing a picnic area. This soon becomes a very rough, very steep track providing a good downhill gallop towards the town. On reaching the surfaced road, continue straight on and follow the road round to the left at the junction, where a small stream comes dashing down on the left. Continue on into the centre of Beaminster.

The view out over Beaminster from Mintern's Hill provides a distant glimpse of the sea.

8 BEAMINSTER TO LYME REGIS

via Pilsdon Pen   *18 miles (29 km)*

Beaminster is an attractive town centred on its market square, with buildings of many periods, but given a sense of unity by the use of local limestone. A circular walk begins from Church Street (see p.136). Leave the square by Church Street and follow it down to the church **39**. The building, as seen today, is mostly 15th century with an immense, elaborately decorated tower. The interior is a little surprising, as the pews have been removed in the modern fashion to be replaced by chairs grouped round an altar in the nave, giving it a somewhat cavernous feeling. The most striking features are two elaborate memorials. Continue past the church down Shorts Lane which leads directly on to a footpath beside a rushing stream. Where the path turns right **A**, continue straight on over the stile into the field and continue the walk beside the water to a stile opposite. At the road, turn left and immediately right down Halfacre Lane. Turn left, just past the last house on the left **B** to take the footpath away from the town.

Cross a stile by a gate and turn diagonally right across the field towards the farm. Beyond the buildings go through a squeeze stile and turn left beside the barn for a path across the field. Soon the next stile

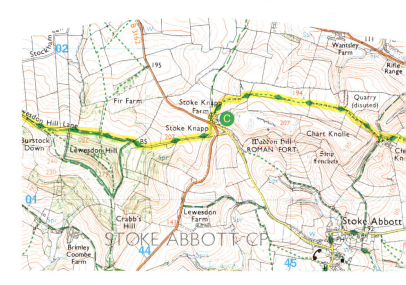

comes into view and very different scenery from that met earlier in the walk appears up ahead. There is no longer the clear demarcation of hills dropping away sharply to valleys and forming long ridges, but instead an irregular pattern of hills and hollows, seemingly arranged at random. The track carries straight on over stiles heading downhill at first, but also heading uncompromisingly for the tallest of the surrounding hills. Head towards a solitary tree and keep going uphill towards a marker post in the hedge. Cross the farm track by two stiles and continue the climb. Although this is a good, long, steep slog, the turf underfoot is soft and the views just keep getting better all the time. The summit **40** has the familiar beech tree crown, and from here one can look down to the left for a glimpse of the sea beyond the hills.

Being a summit, there is an inevitable drop down the other side, but this remains an upland walk over grassland, bright with gorse and flowers. The path leads down past a cosy little farm in a hollow. At the gate by the barns, take the path beside the house. Where paths cross continue straight forward on the broad, green track running round the shoulder of the hill. Reaching two gates, go through the one on the left to follow the field path beside the hedge. At the end of the ridge, take the obvious farm track that leads down towards the road. Go through the farmyard, cross the road and take the bridleway opposite **C**. At first it runs between hedges, then the hedge on the right ends and there is a chance to admire the view. The next climb soon begins and the lane gradually sinks down into the hillside as it heads towards the trees. The track runs round the edge of the wood, and birdsong comes out from

Gerrard's Hill, like many other tops along the way, carries a proud crown of beech trees.

among the trees, ranging from a tuneful warbler to the screeching jay. This is National Trust woodland, predominantly birch and beech, with the track staying near the edge, eventually emerging high above Broadwindsor, providing views from the ridge to rolling farmland on one side and the coastal hills and the sea on the other.

At the road **D**, turn left, then sharp right down the concrete track signposted to Courtwood Farm. Where the surfaced drive swings left, carry straight on along the broad track by the hedge. As the path begins to climb, it becomes a sunken way. At the summit, where tracks meet **E**, turn sharp left to the corner to find two stiles, which are crossed to enter the field on the right. Follow the field path round by the hedge to a stile and cross it to join the farm track, and continue following this round to the left. It goes straight through the farmyard, across a lane, climbing all the time. Where the obvious track peters out at a gate **F** continue up the grassy slope to a marker post, just to the left of a patch of gorse. At the footpath that rims the hill, turn right and immediately left to cross the stile by the National Trust sign for Pilsdon Pen **41**, a hill fort where archaeologists discovered a small goldsmith's workshop – and a Roman ballista, suggesting a turbulent past.

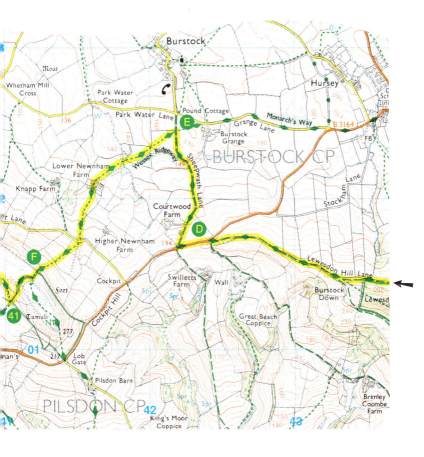

Turn right to follow the path round the ramparts to a fence by a line of gorse and turn downhill on the farm track past a massive beech. The path turns right, going slightly uphill again towards a stile. Once across, turn half left to cross the field, aiming to meet the fence just about at the crest of the ridge. A marker post eventually comes into view at the far corner. Cross two stiles and continue straight forward along the ridge, with a hedge to the right. This is fine, airy walking for a time, continuing straight on in the same direction. At the end of the ridge, where the track begins to go downhill, it swings round to the left and becomes a farm track. At the foot of the hill by a metal gate **G** leave the obvious track which is turning left for a footpath on the right. This leads down the bottom of the field to a gate in the hedge beside the road.

Carry straight on up the road in the same direction to the signpost at Cole's Cross. In spite of the fact that Lyme Regis is the eventual end of the walk, the Way goes in precisely the opposite direction towards Crewkerne. A few paces past the crossroads, turn left through a wooden gate and go uphill to a metal gate close to gorse bushes. The Way now continues along the crest of the ridge, with a view down over a church with a tiny steeple. Stay with the ridge to the far end,

Local building at its best: Grighay Farm.

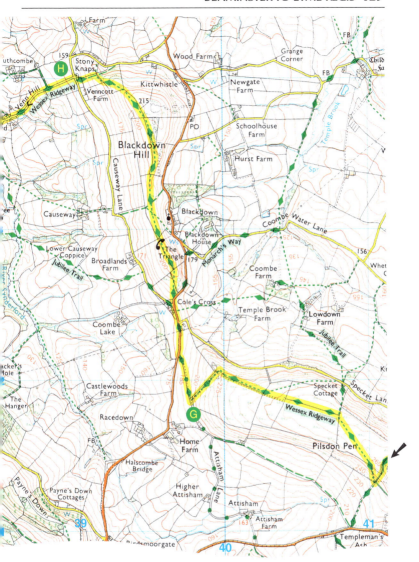

and as the path begins to go downhill, cross a stile and turn half left to the group of trees. Do not cross the stile, but turn left through the metal gate to take the path by the hedge down to the road **H**.

Turn right, then immediately left at the crossroads, on the road signposted to Thorncombe. It goes steadily downhill, past an attractive farm with a duck pond, to a stream, after which there is a steep,

The picturesque grounds of Forde Abbey.

little climb back out of the valley. Turn left at the next road junction **I**, signposted to Saddle Street. The Way has finally turned south, for the last lap down to Lyme. The direction may be seaward, but it is still going uphill. At the farmyard, where paths divide, take the route on the right, still climbing. At the top of the hill, go through a metal gate and turn half left, looking down over the village of Thorncombe to the right. At a path junction **J**, the path does a U-turn to reach a metal gate. Turn right up the next field and follow the path round the edge to find a stile, and then take the path down beside the conifers to the road, with its impressively well-maintained layered hedge **K**. This is the start of a circular walk to Forde Abbey (see p.138).

Turn left along the road and almost immediately right over a pair of stiles to cross a field. At the farm track turn left to pass under the power lines. The wood to the right is full of pheasants that wander nonchalantly out into the fields, blissfully unaware of their possible fate. Pass in front of a particularly good example of a traditional Dorset farmhouse **42**, with an imposing double-storied porch. Turn right onto the farm track and follow it round to the left for a fairly steady descent. Where the track divides, keep to the right, still going downhill. Follow the track as it swings right beside a line of wood, and the next major objective, a high tree-covered hill can be seen up ahead. Go downhill through the farmyard and turn left opposite the house to cross a footbridge over the stream wandering along through the wood. Continue on through a gate and up the hillside to a stile by a gate in the corner of the field. Cross the stream, go past a patch of woodland and bear left towards a gate. Keep following the edge of the field round to the left corner and cross the stile to the road **L**.

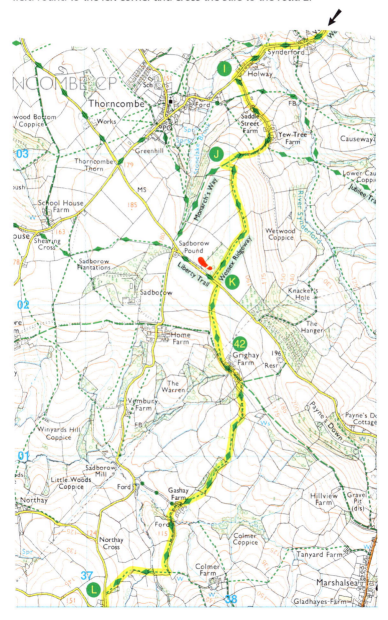

Turn left at the road and carry straight on at the road junction towards Marshwood. Where the road turns left, go straight forward on the rough track that heads steeply uphill to join the road at the edge of the wood. Cross straight over to the road opposite and after a short way turn right **M** for a track climbing steeply up through the woods. At the top, follow the track briefly round the brow of the hill, then turn left through the comparatively small scale ramparts of Lambert's Castle **43**. The walk now leads across the flat, grassy plateau, with no very definite path – or perhaps one should say an excess of paths, for this is an area very popular with locals who have created their own maze of well-trodden ways. In general it keeps near the left hand edge and a pylon provides a useful marker. The track running down from the far side, however, is quite clear, and brings the walk down to a road junction. Continue straight on in the same direction along the road that goes uphill and then follows the crest of the ridge. At the top is Coney's Castle **44** the very last of the Iron Age hill forts met along the way. This one is in the care of the National Trust, and those who want to complete the full hand of forts can reach the top by a path from the car park. Encouragingly, one is now looking directly down to the sea at Charmouth.

Take the road down the hill, and immediately past a junction **N** turn right onto a footpath. Turn half left across the field to head for a stile in the hedge by a large holly tree. Aim for the right hand corner of the large, grassy field and continue straight on in the same direction across the next. Just before reaching the trees, turn right through a gate **O** and follow a path leading towards the left hand side of the nearer group of conifers and then head for the houses.

Turn right along the road and carry straight on at the junction on the road signposted to Monkton Wyld. Immediately over the brow of the hill **P**, turn left onto the track and turn right by the barns. Where the track swings sharp left, carry straight on through the gate on the left and head towards the barn. Go behind the end of the barn to a gap in the hedge and turn half left. Head across the field to a small wooden gate in the hedge just above the woods. This is a very appealing area with wooded hollows and hills bristling with trees.

Keep following the path above the wood, and look out for a stile almost lost among brambles up ahead. The path briefly enters the fringe of woodland, goes downhill and beyond a group of barns, turn left through a gate to follow the line of the stream. Cross over and take a path across stiles that runs between the woods and the stream.

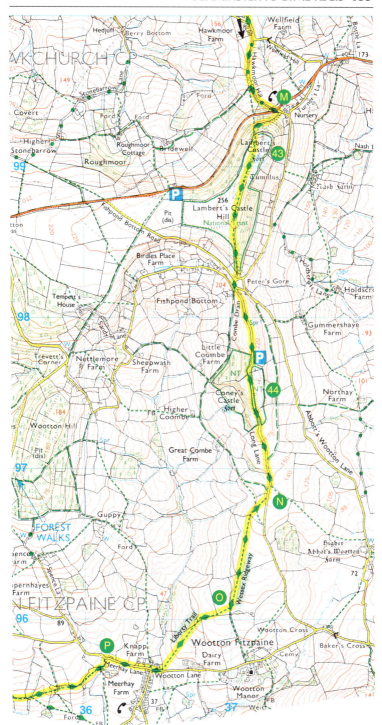

At the farm **Q** turn left by the cow byre onto the track going uphill with woods on the right. Where the way divides by young conifers, turn half right and immediately left. Follow the track up the field to a post where hedges meet and look for a gate by a small ford in the hedge coming up on the left. Cross the next field heading for a gate by a prominent oak and Penn Farm can now be seen. Cross the field heading for the left hand side of the buildings, go through a gate and turn right onto the approach road that leads down to the main road at a lay-by **R**. This is a very busy road, especially during the holiday season, so there can be a long wait before it can be crossed. Go for a few paces down the Lyme road, then turn sharp right onto the bridleway. Reaching a stile, turn left downhill and take the obvious path through the wood. Where tracks divide by a small clearing, carry straight on. Now the track goes downhill at the edge of a large clearing to a gate **S**. Turn left – do not take the footpath across the bridge – and head back into the depths of the conifer plantation. This broader track is soon abandoned for a narrow path running through the trees to the left.

Leaving the woods, cross the stream and take the track uphill towards the houses. Turn left, then right between the houses, and where tracks cross beyond the wooden gate **T** take the path to the right towards the houses spreading up the hillside. These are on the outskirts of Lyme Regis and halfway across the field the sea itself comes into view. The actual introduction to Lyme is, however, rather less romantic, as the path heads downhill through a gap in the woods to emerge at a sewage works **U**.

Turn left onto an attractive waterside path that goes steadily on its way, ignoring the vagaries of the little River Lim. Cross the river by a footbridge below a weir and continue following the riverside walk into Lyme Regis to the sea and the end of a magnificent walk.

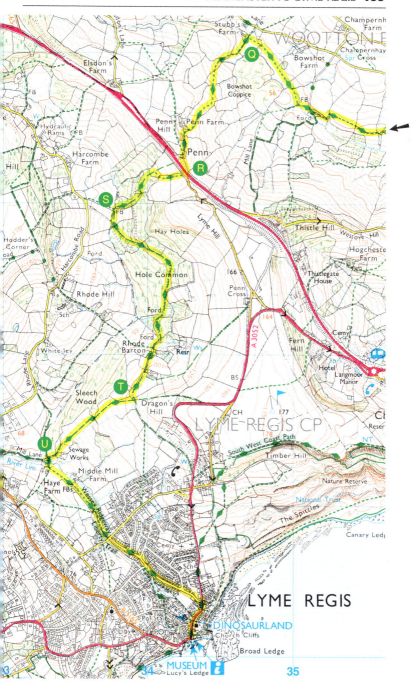

CIRCULAR WALK TO PARNHAM HOUSE

3 miles (5 km)

From the Market Square in Beaminster, go down Church Street, and turn immediately left down St Mary Well Street **A** and continue straight on down the No Through Road that ends at a metal gate. From here a track leads off across the fields with the River Brit down to the left. At the bottom of a grassy hillside crowned with trees take the obvious track signposted to Netherbury. Passing a low bank crowded with ramson, cross the stile to the right of the house and continue on the footpath which turns towards the river bank. The river meanders past parkland and two startling statues of blue suited men come into view, recognisable even at a distance as Morecambe and Wise. The path heads slightly uphill to a stile **B** then turns left back to a bridge over the river and up past the house **38**.

Parnham is a Tudor mansion, very ornate even by the standards of the day, with pinnacles, curlicues, alcoves and Gothic windows. It now houses a furniture-making workshop open to the public and has exhibitions by designers and craftsmen. The walk down the formal avenue to the road passes more sculpture along the way. At the road, turn right and immediately left up the bridleway, through the farmyard, and out the far side to take the rough track beside the surfaced farm road. This sinks down between greensand bluffs like a miniature canyon, with trees spreading their branches overhead as exposed roots creep down the rock face. Nearing the top a strong scent of garlic announces your arrival at a mass of ramson.

The Tudor grandeur of Parnham Manor House.

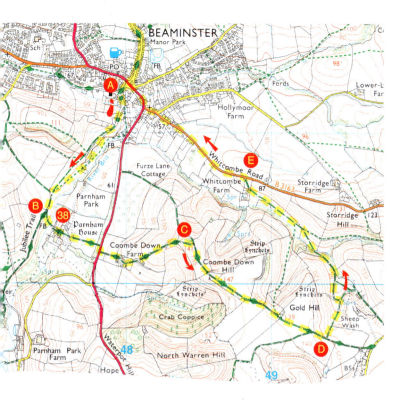

At the top of the steep climb **C** turn right onto the path signposted 'Jubilee Trail'. There is a view out over flat-topped hills as the path follows a prominent ridge, to join a wider track at a metal gate. Continue on past a deep hollow on the right, and beyond a group of barns as the path begins to go downhill again, take the path on the left **D** dropping more steeply down to the valley floor. It comes down to an area of springs and turns left towards the woods, with a stream down to the right. Go through a wooden gate to take the meandering path through the woodland fringe which eventually makes its way down to the gurgling stream, which is crossed on a footbridge. Leave the wood by the gate on the left and carry on past the edge of the woodland to take the path across the face of the grassy hillside towards the houses. Turn right at the farm approach road **E** then left onto the road leading back into Beaminster.

The road leads past a varied and most attractively contrasting set of houses, a homely 17th century cottage stands close by the Georgian elegance of a shell porch and a house with a wrought iron balcony that would not be out of place in New Orleans. Follow the road round to the left to return to the town centre.

CIRCULAR WALK TO FORDE ABBEY

6 miles (9 km)

The route begins where the footpath from Yew Tree Farm meets the road at the end of a conifer plantation **A**. Turn right down the road which reaches an embanked enclosure, Sadborow Pound, where an ornate gateway stands by parkland. At the road junction **B** turn right through a gate to join the obvious broad track running downhill along the side of the field. Near the bottom of the dip, cross over a stile on the left to take the footpath signposted 'Liberty Trail'. It is a narrow tree-shaded lane with a small stream alongside, which cuts its way down to join an ever deeper gorge, with ferns clambering up the banks among the trees. The path opens out to fields on the left, and where the track divides **C** keep to the field-side path on the left, still signposted as 'Liberty Trail'. The village of Thorncombe comes into view in the hollow, below a hillside splashed with the bright yellow of gorse. Where the way divides, leave the waymarked trail for the tree-shaded path on the left.

At the roadway turn right towards the village with its attractive row of flint cottages, and turn immediately left beyond the first cottage **D**. Take the obvious path, overhung by low branches, with a view of the church to the right, with its stumpy, squat tower. Emerging from the trees, take the path to the right of the hedge, with playing fields over to the right. Once past the end of a row of houses keep straight on, heading for the stile in front of the woods. An obvious path leads straight through the conifers, then skirts round the rim of an old pit as a narrow path, not following the more obvious broad track. Continue straight across the next field to the stile opposite and take the obvious path with the tall hedge to the right and head towards the prominent conifers up ahead. Pass Forde Grange Farm with its impressive range of stone barns and cross two stiles to join the road **E**.

Turn right along the road past the farm, then left onto the path by the road junction signposted 'Jubilee Trail'. Go straight across the field by the waymarker posts. Turn left at the edge of the field, then right through the gate. Turn diagonally right towards the corner of the field to reach a stile and turn right onto the road past the gateway to Forde Abbey **F**, an impressive sight with its ornate traceried windows. Cross the three-arched bridge over the modest River Axe. At the road junction, turn left across the stile for a field path alongside the meandering river. A yellow arrow points the way to a footbridge over the river **G**. Once across, turn half left, heading uphill to a stile above the small copse. The route is now back with the Liberty Trail. Turn right at the edge of the field and immediately left to take the obvious track towards the wood to the right of the cottages. Cross straight over the road and across the next field on the path signposted to Forde Abbey Farm. Beyond the farm, cross the stile and turn right up the lane. Where the lane swings right **H** carry straight on to the green track through the woods. Where paths meet two gates, take the one on the left, and turn half right to head for a stile.

Beyond the stile, turn right up the quiet country lane, passing a former small toll booth and turnpike cottage. There is evidence of former importance in the wide road with well cut drainage ditches: now there is not enough traffic to startle the grazing rabbits in the hedgerow. The road leads back to the start.

Scale is approx 2¼ inches to 1 mile

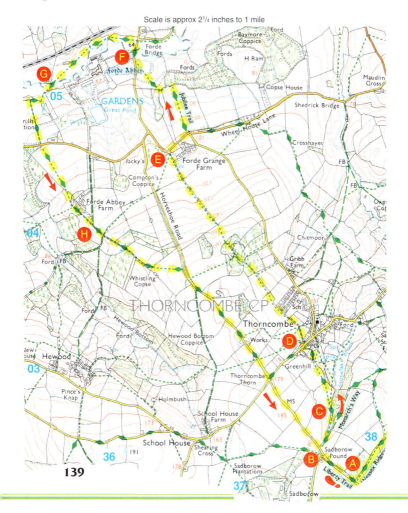

USEFUL
INFORMATION

Transport

Information regarding transport can be obtained from all tourist information centres.

Rail

Passenger rail enquiries: 0345 484950

Marlborough: There is a fast and regular Intercity service from London Paddington which serves Swindon, Chippenham, Pewsey and Bedwyn. There are bus/rail links from Swindon and Bedwyn.

Lyme Regis: There is a bus service from Lyme Regis to the nearest station at Axminster which is on the London Paddington/Exeter Intercity line.

Coach

National Express Enquiries: 0990 808080

Wiltshire County Council Bus Line: 01345 090899

Dorset County Council Passenger Transport Section 01305 225165 (office hours only)

National Taxi Hotline: Freephone 0800 654321

Accommodation

Some bed and breakfast accommodation is given in Stilwell's *National Trail Companion* and *Walk the Wessex Ridgeway in Dorset* by Priscilla Houston, both available from bookshops. Tourist information centres will also provide this information on request. There are no youth hostels on or near the Wessex Ridgeway.

Tourist Information Centres

Avebury
The Great Barn, Avebury, Marlborough SN8 1PF, Tel. 01672 539425

Axminster
The Old Courthouse, Church Street, Axminster, Devon EX13 5AQ, Tel. 01297 34386

Blandford Forum
Marsh & Ham Car Park, West Street, Blandford Forum, Dorset DT11 7AW, Tel. 01258 454770

Devizes
The Crown Centre, 39 St John's Street, Devizes, Wiltshire, SN10 1BL, Tel. 01380 729408

Lyme Regis
Guildhall Cottage, Church Street, Lyme Regis, Dorset, DT7 3BS, Tel. 01297 442138

Marlborough
George Lane Car Park, Marlborough, Wiltshire, SN8 1EE, Tel. 01672 513989

Warminster
Central Car Park, Warminster, Wiltshire, BA12 9BT, Tel. 01985 218548

Westbury
The Library, Edward Street, Westbury, Wiltshire, BA13 3BD, Tel. 01373 827158

USEFUL ADDRESSES

British Trust for Ornithology, The Nunnery, Thetford, Norfolk, IP24 2PU. Tel: 01842 750050.

Countryside Commission, John Dower House, Crescent Place, Cheltenham, Glos, GL50 3RA

Dorset Trust for Nature Conservation, 39 Christchurch Road, Bournemouth, Dorset, BH1 3NS

Dorset Wildlife Trust, Brooklands Farm, Forston, Dorchester, Dorset, DT2 7AA

English Heritage (South West Region) 7-8 King Street, Bristol, BS1 4EQ

English Nature, Prince Maurice Court, Hambleton Avenue, Devizes, Wilts, SN10 2RT

Forestry Commission, Postern Hill Lodge, Marlborough, Wilts SN8 4ND

National Trust, Wessex Regional Office, Eastleigh Court, Bishopstrow, Warminster, Wilts, BA12 9HW

Nature Conservancy Council, Slepe Farm, Arne, Wareham, Dorset, BH20 5BN

Ordnance Survey, Romsey Road, Maybush, Southampton, SO16 4GU

Ramblers Association, 1-5 Wandsworth Road, London SW8 2XX

Royal Society for Nature Conservation, The Green, Witham Park, Waterside South, Lincoln LN5 7JR

Royal Society for the Protection of Birds, The Lodge, Sandy, Beds, SG19 2DL

Wiltshire Wildlife Trust, 19 High Street, Devizes, Wilts, SN10 1AT

ORDNANCE SURVEY MAPS COVERING THE WESSEX RIDGEWAY

Landranger Maps (scale 1:50 000)
173 Swindon & Devizes, Marlborough & Trowbridge
183 Yeovil & Frome
184 Salisbury & The Plain
193 Taunton & Lyme Regis
194 Dorchester, Weymouth & Surrounding Area
195 Bournemouth, Purbeck & Surrounding Area

Explorer Maps (scale 1:25 000)
29 Lyme Regis & Bridport
117 Cerne Abbas & Bere Regis
118 Shaftesbury & Cranborne Chase
130 Salisbury & Stonehenge
143 Warminster & Trowbridge
157 Marlborough & Savernake Forest

Bibliography

Aston, Michael & Lewis, Carenza, *Medieval Landscape of Wessex*, Oxbow Books, 1995

Bettey, J. H., *Wessex From AD 1000*, Longman, 1986

Cunliffe, Barry, *Wessex to 1000 AD*, Longman, 1993

Dorset Wildlife Trust, *The Natural History of Dorset*, The Dovecote Press, 1997

Draper, Jo, *Dorset, The Complete Guide*, The Dovecote Press, 1986

Fowles, John, *A Short History of Lyme Regis*, The Dovecote Press, 1991

Fowles, John & Draper, Jo, *Thomas Hardy's England*, The Dovecote Press, 1984

Hawkins, Desmond, *Cranborne Chase*, The Dovecote Press, 1993

OS Landranger Guide to Dorset, Jarrold, 1987

Reeves, Marjorie, *Sheep Bell & Ploughshare*, Moonraker Press, 1978

Taylor, Christopher, *The Making of the English Landscape: Dorset*, Hodder & Stoughton, 1975

Watts, Kenneth, *The Marlborough Downs*, Ex Libris Press, 1993

Whiteman, Robin, *Wessex*, Weidenfeld & Nicolson, 1994

Wrigley, Chris, *William Barnes, The Dorset Poet*, The Dovecote Press, 1984

Yorke, Barbara, *Wessex in the Early & Middle Ages*, Leicester University Press, 1995

Places to Visit on or near The Wessex Ridgeway

Marlborough
The Merchant's House

Avebury
Avebury Manor and Garden (NT)
Alexander Keiller Museum
The Great Barn

Devizes
Devizes Museum, 41 Long Street
The Canal Centre, The Wharf

* **Westbury**
Heritage Museum

* **Warminster**
Dewey Museum, The Library

* Pythouse
Old Wardour Castle (EH)

Beaminster
Local History Museum, Old Congregational Chapel, Whitcombe Road

* Minterne Gardens

* **Cerne Abbas**
The Abbey

* **Mapperton House and Gardens**

* **Horn Park Gardens**

Lyme Regis
Philpot Museum, Bridge Street
Dinosaurland Fossil World, Coombe St
Marine Aquarium and Cobb History

* Off route